The Missing Link
In
God's Provisions

By
JD Livermore Jr.

Introduction:

The two primary objectives in writing this book are:

#1 To show from scripture that those who are mature in the Word of God and full of the Holy Spirit are called:

A: to be ambassadors of the kingdom of God.

B: to proclaim the good news that the Kingdom of God is available to who-so-ever will believe.

C: to lay hands on the sick and they will recover.

D: to cast out demons setting the captives free.

E: to raise the dead.

F: to do the works that Jesus did and even greater works.

All of this Jesus has commanded we do in His Name that our heavenly Father maybe glorified in the Son.

#2 To enlighten those who need a touch from God to the fact that it comes through those sent in Jesus Name - His ambassadors.

For most believers this book will shed a new light on what Jesus said in: **John 13:20 "Most assuredly, I say to you, he who receives whomever I send receives Me; and he who receives Me receives Him who sent Me." (NKJ)**

This book is not meant to be a work of literary excellence; what my desire is; is to state the truth that God has revealed through His Word as straightforward as possible. Though the language is as simple as possible; the truths laid out in this book are deep; and will be life changing to the truth seeker. I strongly encourage you to have your Bible at hand and a pad to take notes.

This book will revolutionize your faith in God and enlighten you to the authority of an ambassador of Jesus Christ.

DEDICATION

I dedicate this book to my Lord Jesus; it is He who has inspired and enabled me to write this book. And to the faithful disciples of Jesus who are willing to take God at His Word.

And to those who have encouraged me in my walk of faith; I give you my sincere thanks. God bless you.

Table of Contents

CHAPTER ONE

THE AMBASSADOR

1 Corinthians 2:13-14 These things we also speak, not in words which man's wisdom teaches but which the Holy Spirit teaches, comparing spiritual things with spiritual. But the natural man does not receive the things of the Spirit of God, for they are foolishness to him; nor can he know them, because they are spiritually discerned. (NKJ)

Have you noticed that there is a missing link between God, the Provider of all good gifts, and the needs of His people? We can look around us and see God's children suffering at the hand of Satan. We must ask ourselves; why? Why are God's covenant people in such distress, when it is a biblical fact that they have a God who is capable and willing to deliver them from the works of the devil?

I am here to tell you, whether you have noticed or not, there is a missing link in God's provisions. This missing link has happened because there has been, and is a devastating lack of understanding in God's method of ministering through human vessels.

The purpose in writing this book is to identify the need and give directions to the solution. And in Jesus' Name I will do just that.

The missing link in God's provisions is the Spirit Filled man of God. Ambassadors who not only know what authority they have been given in Jesus' Name, BUT who will use that authority as an ambassador for Christ, recognizing the assignment Jesus has given to those who believe in His name.

Note: *Spirit Filled Man refers to mankind - male and female - that has been filled with the Spirit of God.* **Acts 2:17-18 'And it shall come to pass in the last days, says God, that I will pour out of My Spirit on all flesh; your sons and your daughters shall prophesy, your young men shall see visions, your old men shall dream dreams. And on My menservants and on My maidservants I will pour out My Spirit in those days; and they shall prophesy. (NKJ)**

To put it in a nutshell: The Church has forgotten what authority and responsibility a Spirit filled disciple of Jesus has. There are few who know what it means to be an ambassador sent in Jesus' Name. Nor do we know how to receive an ambassador sent in Jesus' Name. My hope is that this study will help change this dilemma we are facing.

In Mark 16:17-18 Jesus said: "And these signs will follow those who believe: In My name they will cast out demons; they will speak with new tongues; "they will take up serpents; and if they drink anything deadly, it will by no means hurt them; they will lay hands on the sick, and they will recover." (NKJ)

As we know the original text of the New Testament scriptures were not written in English but in Greek. Their form of writing does not contain punctuations so it was up to the translators to punctuate. However, we must always interpret scripture with scripture. In so doing; we find that the translator miss-punctuated verse seventeen, the focus should be upon Jesus' name. It should read: **"And these signs will follow those who <u>believe in My name</u>: they will cast out demons; they will speak with new tongues; they will take up serpents; and if they drink anything deadly, it will by no means hurt them; they will lay hands on the sick, and they will recover."**

By allowing scripture to interpret scripture we see this interpretation to be true: **Acts 3:16b ... through faith in His name, has made this man strong, whom you see and know. Yes, the faith which comes through Him has given him this perfect soundness in the presence of you all. (NKJ)**

We see therefore that the Bible clearly teaches us that it is when we have faith in His name that we do His works. **Acts 4:10 "let it be known to you all, and to all the people of Israel, that by the name**

of Jesus Christ of Nazareth, whom you crucified, whom God raised from the dead, by Him this man stands here before you whole. (NKJ)

It is essential that we, Christ's body, know that there is a BIG difference between those who believe and those who believe in the Name of Jesus. In the difference of the punctuation lies the problem we are facing today. There are a whole lot of people who believe, BUT have no idea or understanding of the power that is in the Name of Jesus or the authority an ambassador of Jesus carries.

When Jesus commanded us to go in His Name, He was telling us to go in the fullness of His authority. For the Name of Jesus represents the being to whom the Name Jesus was given. The Name is like a king's signet ring; if you have the authority to use the king's signet ring then you have the king's authority. Likewise, for those who have been baptized into the Name of Jesus. We have been given the right to use the Name of Jesus therefore we have been given His authority and a responsibility to use it as we act on His behalf.

It is possible to believe in Jesus and be saved, yet because we have not understood the duties and responsibilities of being Jesus' ambassadors (that is those sent in His name) we might never exercise the authority that belongs to Jesus as long as we live here on planet earth. My hope is that I may help prevent that from happening by passing on to you what God has revealed to me through His Word. I pray that you will receive revelation of God's will concerning the man of God, the rights and duties of a Spirit filled believer. And that this understanding will flow through the body of Christ as to the importance of receiving God's provisions through His ambassadors.

I do believe this study will be used by God because its foundation is the Word of God. There are far too many teachings in the Church about what man thinks and not enough teaching on what GOD SAID. So let us do as we are instructed in **Romans 3:4 "Let God be true but every man a liar." (NKJ)** If it is a choice between God's Word and the traditions of man we must always choose God's Word!

The truths which are hidden in God's word are the precious treasure that Jesus spoke of in His parable. **Matthew 13:44 "Again, the kingdom of heaven is like treasure hidden in a field, which a man found and hid; and for joy over it he goes and sells all that he has and buys that field. (NKJ)**

If we are not willing to give up the traditions of man there is no way we can obtain the hidden treasures that God has for those who will search them out.

> **Proverbs 25:2 It is the glory of God to conceal a matter, but the glory of kings is to search out a matter. (NKJ)**

Therefore, what I am passing on to you in this book is what the Holy Spirit has revealed to me through the written Word of God not the traditions of men that may not have any biblical foundation. So I challenge you to search the scriptures, "to compare spiritual things with spiritual", to see if what I declare is the truth laid forth in the Word of God or not.

For example; one such unbiblical tradition is that: "God does not desire to operate in the Church today like He did in the early Church." This is a lie and there is no biblical truth to it. It not only lacks truth, it is contrary to scripture. The reason people have come to that conclusion is because they have not witnessed the power of God through Christ's ambassadors in the way God has desired. So this false doctrine is based upon our failure as ambassadors and not upon the authority of God's Word.

Jesus said: **"Go and make disciples ..."** [Matthew 28:19]. So we ask: What is a disciple? A disciple is one who follows in the ways of his master. In the case of the "Christian" far too many are disciples of the "Church" and its ways and not disciples of Jesus and His ways. Now I know; they should be one in the same. The Church should be followers of Jesus' way of being and doing, but to frequent this is not the case. So our evaluation of the Church should be to determine if it is living up to the high calling in Christ Jesus according to the Word of God. The Bible declares that the church which is Christ's body is to be the fullness of Christ [Ephesians 1:22-23]. In other words, if the Church is operating as Christ intended it, then you would be seeing Christ in His fullness as you observe the Church.

The sad reality is we have reduced being Christ-like to a moral issue only. It is a moral issue for sure, but it goes far beyond morality, for Christ was more than a moral being. He is the King of kings and Lord of lords. He is <u>ruler</u> over all and we are called to <u>rule</u> on His behalf using His authority.

1 Corinthians 4:20 For the kingdom of God is not in word but in power. (NKJ)

God's kingdom is not a philosophy but a Spiritual kingdom that is far superior to any other power; spiritual or physical.

God's will is that we use His authority as we operate in the gifts that the Spirit gives the same way the Church did in the book of Acts. We are still the Body of Christ called to do His ministry here on earth today. The same Lord, the same ministry!

Jesus told a parable concerning the kingdom of heaven. This parable declares that He has set us over His affairs while He is away. **Matthew 25:14 "For the kingdom of heaven is like a man traveling to a far country, who called his own servants and delivered his goods to them. (NKJ)**

The parable goes on to declare, Jesus is coming back and we will be required to give an account of how we represented the kingdom of heaven here on earth. Were we faithful with the authority we were given or were we afraid to use it? The answer to that will depend primarily upon our understanding of God's nature. Do we see Him as a good God, one who empowers us to succeed or a harsh God, just waiting to punish?

The Church needs to ask, we need to ask: What are we accomplishing in Jesus' Name? Is it only that which can be done in our own human strength and goodness? Or are we operating in the fullness of Jesus' supernatural authority as the Word admonishes?

In 2 Timothy Chapter three it says, in the last days people will have a form of godliness but denying the power. We are seeing this in the church today; there are some who label anything supernatural of the devil: as if the devil has more power than God.

Jesus' desire has always been that those who are called by His Name minister the provisions that God has made available through the knowledge of the Word and the power of the Holy Spirit for supernatural results. The Word and the Holy Spirit must be combined for either one to be truly effective in us and through us. We can have an abundance of Word knowledge and not much understanding concerning the work of the Holy Spirit and the results will be the lack of faith in the power to put the Word of God to work. Or we can have a good understanding of the power of the Holy Spirit and little knowledge of the Word of God and this will result in limited authority for the Holy Spirit to work on. For the Word is the sword of the Spirit.

I want you to notice in the parable of the kingdom of heaven; Jesus is teaching us that He is the one who does the equipping. It says: **"He delivered his goods to them."** And it goes on to say that He gave to each according to their ability.

The Word and the Holy Spirit is the key in this parable: It says the man called **"his own servants and delivered his goods to them"**. When we receive the Holy Spirit we become God's own children, children who are called to serve God as a loving son serves his father.

So what are the "goods" that Jesus was referring to? They are the very Words of God. In His Words are concealed all the blessings and promises of God. Thank you Lord!

In Romans chapter three the Apostle Paul said that the Jews had an advantage over the gentiles because the Jews had the very Words of God. How much greater then is our advantage under the new covenant today? We not only have the Word of God readily accessible, we also have His Spirit to bring the revelation of the Word.

As we grow in the Word, our responsibility increases to operate in the authority that comes through Jesus; who is the living Word of God. Therefore it is our responsibility to advance the kingdom of light in this dark world.

Forsaking all other gods and falling in love with the Word of God we will find a great treasure unequaled by any other. So, Please! search God's word; there is more treasure to be found. The Holy Spirit is our guide leading us to the treasures contained in God's Word. For in the revealed Word of God is where our love relationship with God is, its birth, its growth, its fulfillment. Outside of the Word there can be no LOVE COVENANT relationship with God.

To Peter, God's Word was a gift that allowed him to walk on water. It also gave him the authority to heal the lame man and so on. What is God's Word doing for you, and through you? Is it taking you beyond the natural into God's kingdom, the supernatural?

Matthew 17 records the concern of Jesus that His disciples understand and operate in the authority given them in His name to overcome the work of Satan. Jesus was fully aware that he would soon be leaving this world and that if the Father's will was to continue being "done on Earth as it is in Heaven", then those who represented Jesus, His ambassadors, would have to perform it.

Matthew 17:14-20 And when they had come to the multitude, a man came to Him, kneeling down to Him and saying, "Lord, have mercy on my son, for he is an epileptic and suffers severely; for he often falls into the fire and often into the water. "So I brought him to Your disciples, but they could not cure him." Then Jesus answered and said, "O faithless and perverse generation, how long shall I be with you? How long shall I bear with you? Bring him here to Me." And Jesus rebuked the demon, and it came out of him; and the child was cured from that very hour. Then the disciples came to Jesus privately and said, "Why could we not cast him out?" So Jesus said to them, "Because of your unbelief; for assuredly, I say to you, if you have faith as a mustard seed, you will say to this mountain, 'Move from here to there,' and it will move; and nothing will be impossible for you. (NKJ)

Did you notice the deep concern of Jesus in this statement? **"O faithless and perverse generation, how long shall I be with you? How long shall I bear with you? Bring him here to Me."**

Jesus was saying: "Look guys, I am not always going to be with you, so when are you going to understand how to operate in the authority that has been given Me? I do not need feeble ambassadors who do not operate in the full authority of My Name."

Jesus' disciples asked: "Why couldn't we cast the demon out?" And Jesus said: "Because of your unbelief." Today we ask the same: "Why can't we cast the demons out and heal the sick and raise the dead?" The answer comes back the same: "Because of your unbelief." We must believe we have the power and authority to do so in Jesus' Name. Remembering that we have Jesus' signet ring, that is the full authority of His Name. We therefore have the responsibility of showing the world just how much authority Jesus has; just like the church in the book of Acts.

Jesus' work on earth was ending; He was not going to be here to declare the good news that the Kingdom of Heaven was available for whosoever would receive it by faith. Nor was He to remain here to lay hands upon the sick and heal them, or to set the captives free and to raise the dead. Jesus was and is depending upon ambassadors to carry on His ministry in the POWER of His Name here on Earth. Jesus was going to the Father where He would see to it that whatever His ambassadors called for in faith would be carried out to the glory of our Heavenly

Father through the name of Jesus. **[John 14:12-13 & Matthew 18:19]**

As we look historically we see that for the first century or two Jesus' ambassadors did a good job of representing the power of Jesus' Name here on Earth. Over time religion took over and we lost the knowledge of the role an ambassador fills in God's kingdom. But there is good news, and that is; the call is still there for those who will believe in the Name of Jesus.

Take **John 14:12-13 "Most assuredly, I say to you, he who believes in Me, the works that I do he will do also; and greater works than these he will do, because I go to My Father. "And whatever you ask in My name, that I will do, that the Father may be glorified in the Son. (NKJ)**

Now notice the last instructions that Jesus gave his ambassadors goes right along with this statement in John 14, again we go back to: **Mark 16:14-20 Later He appeared to the eleven as they sat at the table; and He rebuked their unbelief and hardness of heart, because they did not believe those who had seen Him after He had risen. And He said to them, "Go into all the world and preach the gospel to every creature. "He who believes and is baptized will be saved; but he who does not believe will be condemned. "And these signs will follow those who believe: In My name they will cast out demons; they will speak with new tongues; "they will take up serpents; and if they drink anything deadly, it will by no means hurt them; they will lay hands on the sick, and they** will recover." So then, after the Lord had spoken to them, He was received up into heaven, and sat down at the right hand of God. And they went out and preached everywhere, the Lord working with them and confirming the word through the accompanying signs. Amen. (NKJ) We are called to do the works of Jesus to glorify God. Amen!

Jesus was assigning the responsibilities of His earthly ministry to His ambassadors. And the assignment that Jesus gave that day has not yet been completed. We are still summoned to: **"Go into all the world and preach the gospel to every creature. He who believes and is baptized will be saved; but he who does not believe will be condemned."**

Because we are still on assignment we should have the same signs evident in us today as did the ambassadors of Jesus in the early church: **"And these signs will follow those who believe in My name: they will cast out demons; they will speak with new tongues; they will take up serpents; and if they drink anything deadly, it will by no means hurt them; they will lay hands on the sick, and they will recover."**

Jesus has never told us to ask him to come down from heaven to cast out demons or lay hands on the sick and heal them. What He did say was to go in the power of His Name, which embodies His authority, and proclaim the good news. And for us, His ambassadors, to cast out demons, heal the sick, set the captives free, and raise the dead. Jesus said for us to do those works that He did and even greater works than those. **[John 14: 12]**.

After Peter and John healed the lame man in Jesus' Name, Peter said to the people: "Why do you look at us as if by our own power or godliness we have healed this man?" And Peter went on to say: "It was Jesus' Name and faith in Jesus' Name that healed the Man." **[Acts 3:12-16]**

In other words: It was the authority that belongs to Jesus and our faith in that authority that has healed this man. Peter and John were ambassadors representing Jesus' kingdom and enforcing His will here on earth through their faith filled words.

The power of Jesus' Name alone will not heal, even though it has the power to heal, it must be ministered by a person filled with the Spirit who has faith in the Name of Jesus, and they must be received by a person who has faith to receive healing. That is why the people lined up the sick in the streets so that when Peter passed by his shadow might touch them that they would be healed. Peter carried the authority of Jesus and the faith to use it. **[Acts 5:15-16]**

Consider this: If healing were a matter of prayer only, then there would have been no need for them to receive healing through Peter, they could have prayed on their own and been healed. But throughout history we see that God's provisions have come to those who would recognize the authority invested in His ambassadors.

Acts 14:9-10 Paul, observing him intently and seeing that he had faith to be healed, said with a loud voice, "Stand up straight on your feet!" And he leaped and walked. (NKJ) A winning combination: The man of God and someone who will believe!

After Jesus' departure from earth who did God use to proclaim the Good News, to heal the sick, to deliver the oppressed, to raise the dead? It was and is those sent in Jesus Name, ambassadors of the kingdom of God. They are those who were and are mature in the faith, full of the Word and the Holy Spirit.

Jesus said: *(speaking to his ambassadors)* "<u>You say</u> to the mountain ... and do not doubt in your heart ... and whatsoever <u>you say</u> will be done." [**Mark 11:22-23**] Jesus said it, so we can know that it is God's way of operating. He wants us to go in His Name and speak forth the release of heaven's provisions here on earth. Amen!

We cry out to heaven and ask God to heal us and to deliver us, and God is saying: "Call for My ambassadors, they have the responsibility of doing on My behalf. Is there no one making the Name of Jesus known in word and deed to a needy and hurting world?"

In **James 5:14-15a** it says: **"Is anyone among you sick? Let him call for the elders of the church, and let them pray over him, anointing him with oil in the name of the Lord. And the prayer of faith will save the sick, and the Lord will raise him up."** (NKJ)

The elders are ambassadors in the Name of Jesus to do the works that Jesus would do if He was physically here. The very definition of an Elder is one who is mature in the faith knowing the will of God and full of the Holy Spirit.

It goes on to say in **James 5:16b-18 The effective, fervent prayer of a righteous man avails much. Elijah was a man with a nature like ours, and he prayed earnestly that it would not rain; and it did not rain on the land for three years and six months. And he prayed again, and the heaven gave rain, and the earth produced its fruit. (NKJ)**

Elijah was a man just like us. He was called by God to do the will of God here on earth. When Elijah prayed that it would not rain God manifested according to Elijah's request. When he prayed again, this time for the heavens to give rain, God again moved on Elijah's words. This is the life of an ambassador.

Did not Jesus say: I will do what ever you ask in My name. ?

Isaiah 44:24-26 Thus says the LORD, your Redeemer, and He who formed you from the womb: "I am the LORD, who makes all things, who stretches out the heavens all alone, who spreads abroad the earth by Myself; Who frustrates the signs of the babblers, and drives diviners mad; who turns wise men backward, and makes their knowledge foolishness; <u>Who confirms the word of His servant, and performs the counsel of His messengers;</u> (NKJ)

So we see that today we have two major problems in the Church: The first being there are so few ambassadors who know and have faith to operate in the authority given in Jesus' Name. The second is that those in need of a touch from God do not understand that it comes through a man of God.

God has from the creation of man, without exception, worked here on Earth through mankind, through ambassadors who will do His will here on Earth. Such as: Noah, Abraham, Elijah, Elisha, David, Jesus, Jesus' disciples and so on.

For a perfect example of an ambassador, look at Jesus' ministry here on earth. He came only to do the will of His heavenly Father who sent Him.

Whose will are you doing?

So what made Jesus the perfect ambassador?

Jesus was empowered through the Holy Spirit. **[Luke 3:22]**

Jesus' purpose in life was to do his Father's will, in whose name He was sent. **[Heb.10:7]**

Jesus understood the power of the kingdom He represented. **[Matt.28:18]**

If we follow Jesus' example of being an ambassador we cannot go wrong.

In II Kings Chapter five we find the account of the Syrian commander who was suffering from leprosy. And a Jewish slave girl who knew of a man of God and the authority that he carried as God's man. **II Kings 5:3 Then she said to her mistress, "If only my master were with the prophet who is in Samaria! For he would heal him of his leprosy." (NKJ)**

Just like the Jewish slave girl, we must know where to go to find the provisions of God.

When Jesus was here, the people went to Jesus. Prior to His departure Jesus told us: **"Most assuredly, I say to you, he who receives whomever I send receives Me; and he who receives Me receives Him who sent Me." John 13:20**. **(NKJ)** Think about the magnitude of that declaration from Jesus!

Jesus was declaring that if anyone would accept an ambassador sent in Jesus' Name it would be the same as accepting Jesus himself. The ambassador would have the full authority of Jesus. The truth is, if you receive an ambassador of Jesus you are receiving Jesus, if you receive Jesus you receive His Father who sent Him, for it was in His Father's authority that Jesus came manifesting God's will on earth.

What would be the reaction if Jesus was here on earth today and the word got out about the authority He displayed? People would travel from the farthest reaches of the earth to receive their healing, deliverance, miracles, or to receive His blessing. What if I told you that all that power is accessible in the earth today? The good news from scripture declares that it is here today in His ambassadors, as we have just read in John 13:20.

Jesus was one person and could only be in one place at a time. He said it is for your benefit that I go away, speaking of going to the Father's right hand, for when I go I will send the Holy Spirit to you. By putting the same Spirit that was in Jesus, in His ambassadors, He would be able to minister through many bodies instead of one. His ambassadors have His anointing.

The apostle Paul, an ambassador for Christ, said: "It is no longer I who lives but Christ in me." **[Galatians 2:20]** The Spirit of God was in him and working through him to do God's will here on earth. Is that anointing evident in us today?

Even though we have the Spirit of God living in us we still must release that power by faith. And faith comes through intimacy with the Word of God.

Again, it is the purpose of this book that the Saints may be built up in their faith through the Word so that they can release the provisions of God to a needy and hurting world, glorifying God in the process.

Have you surrendered your own personal ambitions to become an ambassador for Jesus? And are you willing, through faith in the Name of Jesus, to release God's provisions?

Jesus said: **Matthew 10:39 "He who finds his life will lose it, and he who loses his life for My sake will find it. (NKJ)**

This is an invitation from Jesus to lay down your life and take up His cause that the kingdom of heaven may be advanced here on earth. If we will lay down our life, we will find our true worth and become truly alive, spiritually alive. There is no greater joy than to find your life in the will of God. Amen!

AMBASSADORS MUST LET GOD'S WORD DEFINE WHO THEY ARE!

This is a big problem for most of us, we have let "the world" define us, therefore we see ourselves as "the world" sees us. STOP! We are no longer of the world, we are called to be a reflection of the Son, Jesus. We must learn to see ourselves in His likeness, only then will we be suitable ambassadors of the kingdom of God.

In Acts chapter three we see a man in need and men who knew who they were in Christ; ambassadors. Knowing the authority and the responsibilities they had in Jesus' name they reflected His glory by making the kingdom power known to a lame man.

Acts 3:2-8 And a certain man lame from his mother's womb was carried, whom they laid daily at the gate of the temple which is called Beautiful, to ask alms from those who entered the temple; who, seeing Peter and John about to go into the temple, asked for alms. And fixing his eyes on him, with John, Peter said, "Look at us." So he gave them his attention, expecting to receive something from them. Then Peter said, "Silver and gold I do not have, but what I do have I give you: In the name of Jesus Christ of Nazareth, rise up and walk." And he took him by the right hand and lifted him up, and immediately his feet and ankle bones received strength. So he,

leaping up, stood and walked and entered the temple with them—walking, leaping, and praising God. (NKJ)

Peter said, **"Silver and gold I do not have, but what I do have I give you: In the name of Jesus Christ of Nazareth, rise up and walk."** What Peter had was the provisions of God in him through the abiding presence of the Holy Spirit and the Word. And what the man needed was the ability to walk, which he had never had from birth. By faith, Peter released the supernatural provision of God to meet the man's need. I am sure that pleased God and brought glory to His Name. And that is doing the work of the one you represent, that is being an ambassador.

Throughout New Testament history there has been a remnant of Jesus' disciples who have been ministering to those in need through the supernatural power of the kingdom of God. The kingdom Jesus has established and is establishing through those who put their faith in the Name of Jesus.

Remember: A true ambassador never seeks his own will or glory, but his whole purpose is to do the will of the one he represents. In so doing the power he represents stands behind what he says, for he only declares the will of the one who sent him.

Jesus said: "I only speak what I hear my Father speak." **[John 8:28]** Are we hearing what God is saying and are we speaking it with authority?

The ambassador who represents the strongest power has the advantage over all other powers. That is good news for Christ's ambassadors, for we represent the kingdom that is above all powers. None can compare. Praise God!

1 Peter 4:11 If anyone speaks, let him speak as the oracles of God. If anyone ministers, let him do it as with the ability which God supplies, that in all things God may be glorified through Jesus Christ, to whom belong the glory and the dominion forever and ever. Amen. (NKJ)

The truth is God has said that if we speak as an ambassador it is the same as God himself speaking. All principalities and powers must take notice and bow to the authority we represent. There is no name that is not subject to the Name of Jesus.

The Bible teaches; that if you see a man in need and have the means to provide for that need then do so. Now the man of God has within him the provisions and authority of God, so we do have the means.

Jesus said: **Luke 17:21b For indeed, the kingdom of God is within you." (NKJ)**

When we receive the Holy Spirit we receive the kingdom of God within us. There is nothing more this world needs than what is in a Spirit filled man of God. Can you shout HALLELUJAH!?

Jesus said in **John 16:13-15 "However, when He, the Spirit of truth, has come, He will guide you into all truth; for He will not speak on His own authority, but whatever He hears He will speak; and He will tell you things to come. "He will glorify Me, for He will take of what is Mine** and declare it to you. "**All things that the Father has are Mine. Therefore I said that He will take of Mine and declare it to you. (NKJ)**

And in Ephesians chapter one the apostle Paul prays that we might understand all that is in us, that is to understand that the kingdom of God is in us - that through our covenant relationship with God we are now coheirs of the kingdom of God with Jesus.

As covenant partners in the kingdom of God we have a call on our life to be ambassadors of the Word of God; to show the power and authority that is in the Name of Jesus as we minister to a hurting and suffering world.

1. We have an assignment to do Christ's ministry here as Ambassadors. **[John 14:12]**
2. All the provisions of God are within the man of God. **[Luke 17:21]**
3. As Spirit filled believers everything we do is to be done in the Name of Jesus. **[Colossians 3:17]**
4. The sick has been instructed to call for Christ's ambassadors. **[James 5:14]**

Bring Glory to God by using Jesus' authority to defeat every enemy that exalts itself against the Word of God!

Now to help the body of Christ dig deep in their pursuit of understanding the calling that is upon the ambassadors of Christ, we will now move to the basic truths about God. So that your faith may be built upon the Rock; which is the Word of God, and not on the traditions of men. For if we are not willing to let go of the traditions of men then we will not be able to take hold of the truths that is found in the Word of God.

Now let us go deeper, that we might go higher, and only then can we make a wider impact as ambassadors sent in Jesus' Name. Can you say amen?

CHAPTER TWO

GOD AND HIS AUTHORITY

Isaiah 46:9-10 Remember the former things of old, for I am God, and there is no other; I am God, and there is none like Me, Declaring the end from the beginning, and from ancient times things that are not yet done, saying, 'My counsel shall stand, and I will do all My pleasure,' (NKJ)

Since this book is primarily a study of our spiritual authority; it would only make sense that we seek to understand the Giver of all authority. Who is He? He is the one and only true God, the Creator of all things. The origin of all authority is our Creator God. If we do not understand the magnitude of God and His authority there is no way we can operate in the fullness of the authority given to us in His Name.

Therefore, let us prepare ourselves through the Word of God, to understand the will of God regarding

His delegated authority to man. Only then will we be properly prepared ambassadors of the kingdom of God here on earth.

Remember; the Bible says that we are in the world but we are not of this world, we are to live here as foreigners representing our home land; God's Kingdom. **[John 17: 14-16]**.

When ambassadors are sent in the name of their government it is needful for them to understand just how much authority, power and resource, their government has. If not, there is no way that they can represent their government properly. They will without a doubt end up allowing their adversary to keep ground that they have no right to. Likewise, we represent the Kingdom of God here on this planet earth, so let us be diligent in our pursuit of knowledge of the ways of our King and His kingdom that we may represent Him in a way that is keeping with His Supreme Authority. Amen

This chapter will set the foundation upon which we can build our understanding of what it means to be an ambassador of the kingdom of God.

GOD IS ALMIGHTY

God said in **Revelation 1:8 "I am the Alpha and the Omega, the Beginning and the End," says the Lord, "who is and who was and who is to come, the <u>Almighty</u>." (NKJ)** This whole verse rings with the superiority of God, but for now I would like for us to focus on the adjective "Almighty" that describes the authority and power of God.

- **Almighty** means: Having absolute power, being superior to all other powers.

Another definition for Almighty is: Our Creator God, the Alpha and Omega. The word almighty defines Him and He defines it, for He is the only one that the name Almighty can be applied to in the complete meaning of the word!

Now don't rush through this truth, as elementary as it might seem. Make sure you believe this with all your heart; meditate on this truth. Because if you know with all certainty that our God is the Almighty One then no matter what comes against you, you will know that in the might of His Name you have authority over it.

As ambassadors we are covenant members of the Kingdom of God; therefore we are under the protection and provisions of that Kingdom. Whatever resources it takes to assure that we receive all that our King has promised to us will be provided according to our faith. Nothing can hold back God's promises for those who are of His Kingdom - except unbelief - because our God is the Almighty One.

Hebrews 6:12 ... through faith and patience *(we)* inherit the promises. (NKJ)

Jesus said in **John 16:33 "These things I have spoken to you, that in Me you may have peace. In the world you will have tribulation; but be of good cheer, I have overcome the world." (NKJ)**

Praise God! It is in Jesus' victory "that we live, and move and have our being". Our strength lies in our faith in what Jesus has already done and in the authority of His Almighty Name. For His authority is our authority, in that, He has given us His Name.

I John 5:5 Who is he who overcomes the world, but he who believes that Jesus is the Son of God? (NKJ) Through faith in Jesus' authority we are more than conquerors!

GOD IS ALL KNOWING

It is a fact that whoever has the most power is the Almighty One. God is that and more. God is not only the Almighty One; He also possesses all knowledge and wisdom. No one can outsmart or manipulate God because all wisdom and knowledge comes from Him. All that any other being can do is to discover what God already knows. And His knowledge and wisdom lives in us through the abiding presence of His Spirit. And through His Holy Spirit He is able to reveal to us the deep and hidden things that only God alone knows.

John 16:13 "However, when He, the Spirit of truth, has come, He will guide you into all truth; for He will not speak on His own authority, but whatever He hears He will speak; and He will tell you things to come. (NKJ)

The Holy Spirit that lives in us knows ALL truth. AND if we will seek truth, He will guide us into <u>all</u> truth. He is the one who shows us the deep and hidden things of God. BUT we must be seeking; for a ship that is not moving cannot be guided by its rudder. It is our responsibility to seek and the Holy Spirit's responsibility to guide.

God not only knows all that has happened, He also knows all that will happen. There is no other being that knows and holds the future in His power. Praise God, for He is the only one worthy!

Isaiah 46:9-10 Remember the former things of old, for I am God, and there is no other; I am God, and there is none like Me, Declaring the end from the beginning, and from ancient times things that are not yet done, saying, 'My counsel shall stand, and I will do all My pleasure,' (NKJ)

There is none like our God; He has declared the end from the beginning. We may not know what tomorrow will bring, but we can know Him who holds tomorrow in His incorruptible authority. And when we need to know tomorrow beforehand God will make it known to us. This too is part of the job of an ambassador, to make known what God is about to do.

EVERYTHING IS SUBJECT TO ITS CREATOR

In the conversation that God was having with Job, God makes it very clear that He alone is responsible for all creation. And that He had no advisers, nor did He have need of any. His wisdom and understanding was complete and lacked nothing.

Job 38:4-12 "Where were you when I laid the foundations of the earth? Tell Me, if you have understanding. Who determined its measurements? Surely you know! Or who stretched the line upon it? To what were its foundations fastened? Or who laid its cornerstone, when the morning stars sang together, and all the sons of God shouted for joy? "Or who shut in the sea with doors, when it burst forth and issued from the womb; When I made the clouds its garment, and thick darkness its swaddling band; When I fixed My limit for it, and set bars and doors; When I said, 'This far you may come, but no farther, and here your proud waves must stop!' "Have you commanded the morning since your days began, and caused the dawn to know its place, (NKJ)

God goes on to help Job understand that He knows what He is doing. So when we do not understand what is going on we can trust that God does, and take comfort in that, until we receive understanding, like Job did.

And in the book of John it also testifies to the fact that our God is the Creator of all. **John 1:1-4 In the beginning was the Word, and the Word was with God, and the Word was God. He was in the beginning with God. All things were made through Him, and without Him nothing was made that was made. In Him was life, and the life was the light of men. (NKJ)**

Our God is so powerful that all He did was speak and from nothing except His Almighty power and His Word we see that all of creation was created by Him, both the seen and unseen.

Creation account goes like this:

1. God our heavenly Father designed all creation.
2. Then the Word was spoken.
3. Upon the Word the Holy Spirit acted, performing what had been spoken.

In creation was a triune God working in complete unity to create. Because God created all and is almighty, He is therefore the supreme Ruler over all. Amen.

Note: As we learn from creation: The Holy Spirit only manifests according to the authority of the Word. So if you want the Holy Spirit to be powerful in your life, then operate in the authority of God's Word.

Now consider this: Something cannot come from nothing. This is a truth to ponder and to share with unbelievers in the hope that they may see the God of creation, the only true God and come into a relationship with Him through Jesus.

Even those who support the evolution theory believe that there was something that caused the "big bang" that set everything in motion. They are without a doubt wrong in their theory but I do agree that all we see and understand had to come from something. The only reasonable explanation is there is a Creator God who has perfect wisdom and unequaled power. He calculated the "end from the beginning" without one error. He never had to say, stop everything while I fix a glitch in the system. What an awesome God!

Let us use the faculties that we have to reason. If God had not always existed then how could anything else exist? Nothing plus nothing always equals nothing. But God plus nothing equals all that has been created, seen and unseen.

$0 + 0 = 0$

God $+ 0 =$ All creation, seen and unseen!

Isaiah 45:18 For thus says the LORD, who created the heavens, who is God, who formed the earth and made it, who has established it, who did not create it in vain, who formed it to be inhabited: "I am the LORD, and there is no other. (NKJ)

Revelation 4:11 "You are worthy, O Lord, to receive glory and honor and power; for You created all things, and by Your will they exist and were created." (NKJ)

Colossians 1:15-17 *(Speaking of Jesus it says:)* **He is the image of the invisible God, the firstborn over all creation. For by Him all things were created that are in heaven and that are on earth, visible and invisible, whether thrones or dominions or principalities or powers. All things were created through Him and for Him. And He is before all things, and in Him all things consist. (NKJ)**

The TRUTH is that God has always existed and that He is the source of all things. There is no other explanation for creation that can truthfully and fully explain it. So if you cannot accept the Creator by faith, through the Word of God, and the evidence of creation itself then you do not believe in the eternal Truth, God! Which means this book may not be for you.

This book is for those who will take God at His Word. His Word is the eternal truth that can never be altered and has no flaws, no weaknesses. Because it is truth it will remain forever, all other theories that do not agree with the Word of God, however, will pass away.

A lie might be able to hide the truth for a time but it can in no way alter it, for truth by nature is eternal.

If you know God's Word, you know the truth, and if you know the truth you know God.

The Bible clearly states that creation itself testifies that there is a Creator and it testifies of His qualities. **Romans 1:20 For since the creation of the world His invisible attributes are clearly seen, being understood by the things that are made, even His eternal power and Godhead, ... (NKJ)**

How can anyone look at all the evidence that creation provides and still say that it happened by chance, that there was not a great design to all creation? All we have to do is look at the complex DNA in the simplest forms of life for evidence of a Creator God. Only a fool says: "There is no God."

The word God is not a name but a description, "a title" of the being we're referring to. Such an example would be the title "father". This is not your father's name but one word to describe his position in the family. So it is with "God".

The term "God" is "Self existing, self sufficient one".

The God of the Bible, the God of creation, is the only true God. As we seen in Job and in John chapter one all things came from our God, so that disqualifies every other being from that position. Our God alone is self existing, and all things depend upon him for existence.

God not only created all things but by His power all things are held together. Therefore, if God ceased to exist so would everything He created.

Colossians 1:16-17 For by Him all things were created that are in heaven and that are on earth, visible and invisible, whether thrones or dominions or principalities or powers. All things were created through

Him and for Him. And He is before all things, and <u>in</u> Him all things consist. (NKJ)

The word "consist" means "to hold together". <u>In Christ all things are held together.</u>

If it were possible to destroy God; now we know it is NOT possible for He is not subject to anything but himself, but if it were, when God ceased to exist so would all things, seen and unseen.

Colossians 1:13-17 He has delivered us from the power of darkness and conveyed us into the kingdom of the Son of His love, in whom we have redemption through His blood, the forgiveness of sins. He is the image of the invisible God, <u>the firstborn over all creation</u>. <u>For by Him all things were created that are in heaven and that are on earth, visible and invisible, whether thrones or dominions or principalities or powers. All things were created through Him and for Him. And He is before all things, and in Him all things consist.</u> (NKJ)

No other being can boast such a claim and be telling the truth. God alone, the Alpha and the Omega has the say over all, whether seen or unseen.

This truth is evident in the fact that God will judge all beings on judgment day. You can not judge anything that you do not have authority over. That is why a foreign ambassador cannot be judged by our courts even if he breaks our law. He is not subject to our courts.

You can only judge what is under your authority.

Romans 14:4a & 10-12 Who are you to judge another's servant? To his own master he stands or falls. ... But why do you judge your brother? Or why do you show contempt for your brother? For we shall all stand before the judgment seat of Christ. For it is written: "As I live, says the Lord, every knee shall bow to Me, and every tongue shall confess to God." So then each of us shall give account of himself to God. (NKJ)

If God was not the ultimate authority He would be the one judged and not the one judging. BUT the fact is that He is the final judge, what He says stands. God cannot be overruled, for He is Truth and truth stands supreme.

Aren't you glad that we, who have been united with Christ, will be judged according to His righteousness? It is He who loved us enough to die for us. Thank you Lord! **[Romans. 8: 33-39]**

GOD NEVER GOES BACK ON HIS WORD

The truth about our God is that He <u>never</u> goes back on His word. He is right and just in all that He says, so when God speaks it becomes law and it can never be altered. His words are eternal. **Matthew 24:35 "Heaven and earth will pass away, but My words will by no means pass away. (NKJ)**

A good example of an established law is found in **Daniel 6:8 "Now, O king, establish the decree and sign the writing, so that it cannot be changed, according to the law of the Medes and Persians, which does not alter." (NKJ)**

The law of the Medes and Persians could not be altered; then how much more so God's word?

The Bible says in **Numbers 23:19 "God is not a man, that He should lie, nor a son of man, that He should repent. Has He said, and will He not do? Or has He spoken, and will He not make it good? (NKJ)**

And according to **Hebrews 6:18 ...it is impossible for God to lie... (NKJ)** Notice it does not say that God <u>will not</u> lie. No, there is a much greater truth here than that, it being that it is <u>impossible</u> for God to lie. We need to get a hold of this!

It is impossible for God to lie because there is nothing false in him. God is God and what ever He speaks His Spirit acts upon and carries it out to fulfillment.

Here is an example: If God were to say; "From this moment on all humans shall be green in color", the Spirit of God would then act on that decree and all humans would be green in color. There would be no debate over whether it is possible or whether it would be a good idea. If God were to say it, it would be done and no one could change it, <u>not even God</u>.

That is the authority that God used at the Tower of Babel. **[Genesis 11:7]** God said: Let their language be confused so that they do not all speak the same language. And what happened? The Spirit, the power of God, come upon them and confused their language, and from that time on there has been many languages. God's Word cannot be altered.

Be assured there is no other power or authority that can prevent what God says from coming to pass, for God is supreme. He is the Almighty God.

It is impossible for God to lie because:

1. There is nothing false in God.
2. What ever God says the Spirit performs.
3. God never misspeaks Himself.

God said: **Isaiah 46:10b 'My counsel shall stand, and I will do all My pleasure,' (NKJ)**

It is very important that we understand what God says rules and that God NEVER changes His mind. Then we will know that what God has said in the past is just as authoritative today as the day He spoke it. The Word of God is the same yesterday, today and forever. **[Hebrews 13:8]**.

Now with the Medes and Persians referred to in the Book of Daniel, they would not resend a law, but they could be and were overthrown by a stronger power and their laws were discarded and replaced with the laws of the new ruling power.

Not so with God, He reigns far above all other principalities and powers. The fact is that He was the one who created them and He will judge them. His throne is FAR above all other principalities and powers, in the heavens, on the earth or under the earth. Amen.

NOTE: WE ARE GOD'S REALITY; GOD IS NOT OUR REALITY.

Even if we choose to create a false reality and deny God it does not change the fact that we are still a part of God's reality and we will all answer to Him. So why not live up to the high calling that God has placed upon us who are called by His Name, and fully enjoy our position in Christ Jesus?

Many "Christians" in their lack of understanding of God have created a false image of Him. This is why we need to allow the Word of God to show us who the one true God is, that we might see Him as He really is, and see ourselves in His reality which is His Word.

Luke 4:4 But Jesus answered him, saying, "It is written, 'Man shall not live by bread <u>alone</u>, but by every word of God.'" (NKJ) The word translated <u>alone</u> is the Greek word monos; and it implies "mere". So we could read Luke 4:4 this way: "It is written, 'Man shall not live by mere bread, but by every word of God.'"

God's words have framed our reality and we cannot go outside of that framework. But within God's reality we have much freedom to create our own reality. God created us with a freewill, and it is His desire that we would honor Him with it. God does not want us as slaves; He desires our obedience through a covenant of love. That is: God loving us; as we respond in obedience to His love. Jesus said: If we love Him we will live our life in agreement with His words. **[John 14:15]**

We can choose to trust in what God says and live accordingly, and if we do we will live up to the high calling that God has placed upon those called by His Name. Or we can put our trust in "other gods" and find ourselves living under the influence of Satan. Living in a lesser reality and reaping the rewards of that reality instead of receiving the blessings that God desires for us.

II Thessalonians 2:9-12 The coming of the lawless one is according to the working of Satan, with all power, signs, and lying wonders, and with all unrighteous deception among those who perish, <u>because they did not receive the love of the truth,</u> that they might be saved. And for this reason God will send them <u>strong delusion,</u> that they should believe the lie, that they all may be condemned who did not believe the truth but had pleasure in unrighteousness. (NKJ)

"Strong delusion" means that they will be living in a reality that Satan has designed for them that denies the truth of God's Word.

In God's reality there is the realm of blessings and the realm of curses and we have to choose in which realm we are going to live. We cannot take the blessings with us where ever we choose; we must stay in the realm of the blessings. And they are found in obedience to the Word of God.

Read Deuteronomy Chapter 28. It explains the blessings and curses that are based upon our decisions to obey God.

Deuteronomy 30:19-20 "I call heaven and earth as witnesses today against you, that I have set before you life and death, blessing and cursing; therefore choose life, that both you and your descendants may live; "that you may love the LORD your God, that you may obey His voice, and that you may cling to Him, for He is your life .... (NKJ)

Concluding statement for this chapter: God was before all, and through Him all thing were created, first spiritual, for God is spirit and then matter, the physical worlds and everything in them. And His Word is above all other authority; it always has been and always will be, for everything exists in and through the power of His Word. God is God and there is no other.

1. There is only one being who is God for God is self-existing and self-sufficient. **[Isaiah 46:9-10]**
2. The evidence that God exists is in creation itself. **[Romans 1:20]**
3. Because God created all, He is over all, and subsequently judge of all. **[John 8:50]**

4. God's Word is law and it is irrevocable. **[Matthew 24:35]**
5. God cannot lie because the Spirit performs whatever is spoken by God. **[Genesis 1:3]**
6. God knows and has declared the end from the beginning. **[Isaiah 46:10]**
7. God + nothing = all creation, seen and unseen. **[Colossians 1:13-17]**

Now to know God like this should give us confidence that no matter what we are facing or will face the authority given to God's ambassadors in the Name of Jesus is greater by far than the authority of the principalities and powers that come against us.

ASSURANCE IS: KNOWING WE CAN COUNT ON GOD'S WORD! "All other ground is sinking sand."

Bring Glory to God by using Jesus' authority to defeat every enemy that exalts itself against the Word of God!

CHAPTER THREE

MAN'S AUTHORITY AND ITS ORIGIN

Genesis 1:26-27 Then God said, "Let Us make man in Our image, according to Our likeness; let them have dominion over the fish of the sea, over the birds of the air, and over the cattle, over <u>all</u> the earth and over every creeping thing that creeps on the earth." So God created man in His own image; in the image of God He created him; male and female He created them. (NKJ)

"**G**OD SAID" Therefore, we need to apply everything we have learned about God and His authority to those two words.

For the more we understand about God and His nature the more significant those two words become. And the more we understand the authority behind

53

those words, the more we understand what authority man was created for.

Our authority is linked directly to God's authority. For God planned that mankind from their first breath was ruler over the earth and all that is in it, upon it, and over it.

God is the designer; supplier; and builder of all creation. He created man in His likeness and in His image to be the ruler over all the earth. It was God who said: **"Let Us make man in Our image, according to Our likeness; let them have dominion over the fish of the sea, over the birds of the air, and over the cattle, over all the earth and over every creeping thing that creeps on the earth."** Man did not appoint himself ruler over the earth, nor could he, only God has that authority.

Psalms 115:16 declares: **"The heaven, even the heavens, are the LORD'S; but the earth He has given to the children of men." (NKJ)** The earth belongs to God and through His sovereignty He chose to give dominion to mankind.

God Himself refers to us as the gods of this earth: **John 10:34 Jesus answered them, "Is it not written in your law, 'I said, "You are gods" '? (NKJ)**

As we consider the fact that mankind was made in the image and likeness of God Himself, how else could we be described? Our very makeup is that of God. He created us in the image and likeness of the King of kings and the Lord of lords.

We will see throughout this book that we were made in the image and likeness of God, therefore, we have the ability to speak things into existence.

Because of our God-like nature whatever we speak will be producing; good or evil. That is why the Bible declares that it is by our words that we will be judge. [Matt. 12: 36-37]. In a later chapter we will explore the power of our words more thoroughly and in depth in the Word of God.

In the beginning, Adam and Eve had no physical labor; they produced according to their words. [Genesis 1:28] Remember, they were created to rule in the same pattern as their God. It was only after their willful disobedience against God's Word that they were condemned to work physically.

Genesis 3:17-19 Then to Adam He said, "Because you have heeded the voice of your wife, and have eaten from the tree of which I commanded you, saying, 'You shall not eat of it': "Cursed is the ground for your sake; in toil you shall eat of it all the days of your life. Both thorns and thistles it shall bring forth for you, and you shall eat the herb of the field. In the sweat of your face you shall eat bread till you return to the ground, for out of it you were taken; for dust you are, and to dust you shall return." (NKJ)

It was through Adam's sin that the earth came under a curse. Corruption extended to all that was under their jurisdiction. For God had placed all the earth under man's dominion. And this condition of ongoing perversion is evident today as a result of man speaking words that rebel against God's Word.

It is possible for man to cause damage with his hands; however it is limited. But with his mouth; he has the power of even life and death, to create or to destroy.

When God said that we were made in His image and likeness He was not referring to our physical appearance, for God is Spirit. **John 4:24 "God is Spirit, and those who worship Him must worship in spirit and truth."(NKJ)** And until Jesus was conceived in Mary's womb God did not have a physical body. **John 1:14 And the Word became flesh and dwelt among us, and we beheld His glory, the glory as of the only begotten of the Father, full of grace and truth. (NKJ)**

So we were created as a spirit who has a soul and lives in a body, we are a triune being just like our Creator God. When we live according to the way God designed us, all three should flow in unity. Our spirit searches the things of God and ministers to our soul. Our soul then instructs our body which in turn speaks forth what originated in our spirit. Then from the fruit of our lips we eat.

1 Corinthians 2:9-13 But as it is written: "Eye has not seen, nor ear heard, nor have entered into the heart of man the things which God has prepared for those who love Him." But God has revealed them to us through His Spirit. For the Spirit searches all things, yes, the deep things of God. For

what man knows the things of a man except the spirit of the man which is in him? Even so no one knows the things of God except the Spirit of God. Now we have received, not the spirit of the world, but the Spirit who is from God, that we might know the things that have been freely given to us by God. These things we also speak, not in words which man's wisdom teaches but which the Holy Spirit teaches, comparing spiritual things with spiritual. (NKJ)

Far too often we get it turned around by allowing our flesh, the sin nature, to rule us. We allow our flesh to dictate to our soul causing us to set our heart on the things of the world. We then start talking like the world, reaping a harvest of corruption.

Romans 8:5-6 For those who live according to the flesh set their minds on the things of the flesh, but those who live according to the Spirit, the things of the Spirit. For to be carnally minded is death, but to be spiritually minded is life and peace. (NKJ)

God gave us a spirit and it is through our spirit that we are able to relate with Him, for spiritual things can only be discerned by the Spirit. And so it is that God desires to relate to His children on a spiritual level, on His level, that we might know Him more intimately.

1 Corinthians 2:14-15 But the natural man does not receive the things of the Spirit of God, for they are foolishness to him; nor can he know them, because they are spiritually discerned. But he who is spiritual judges all things, yet he himself is rightly judged by no one. (NKJ)

But we are more than spirit; we are also a soul, for our soul is the wellspring that produces the fruit of our life. The soul is often referred to as the heart of man.

Luke 6:45 "A good man out of the good treasure of his heart brings forth good; and an evil man out of the evil treasure of his heart brings forth evil. <u>For out of the abundance of the heart his mouth speaks.</u> (NKJ)

And, **Proverbs 18:20-21 A man's stomach shall be satisfied from the fruit of his mouth, from the produce of his lips he shall be filled. Death and life are in the power of the tongue, and those who love it will eat its fruit. (NKJ)**

Let us come back to God's original blueprint for man. God did not create man without a specific purpose in mind. God's intent was to create a man who would rule and reign over His creation; as he walked with his God. And because this man was to rule like God rules he would do so by the power of his words. And God's intent for us today is the same.

God said, "Let Us make man in Our image, according to Our likeness; <u>let them have dominion</u> over the fish of the sea, over the birds of the air, and over the cattle, <u>over all the earth</u> and over every creeping thing that creeps on the earth."

Just as the Pharaoh of Egypt gave his authority to Joseph to rule over his kingdom so God has given His authority over the earth to mankind.

Genesis 41:41-44 And Pharaoh said to Joseph, "See, I have set you over all the land of Egypt." Then Pharaoh took his signet ring off his hand and put it on Joseph's hand; and he clothed him in garments of fine linen and put a gold chain around his neck. And he had him ride in the second chariot which he had; and they cried out before him, "Bow the knee!" So he set him over all the land of Egypt. Pharaoh also said to Joseph, "I am Pharaoh, and without your consent no man may lift his hand or foot in all the land of Egypt." (NKJ)

Because the Pharaoh possessed full authority over the land of Egypt and its inhabitancy, he had the undisputed right to give authority to whoever he chose. According to these scriptures Joseph was given full authority over the land of Egypt. Joseph was not answerable to anyone except the Pharaoh himself. And it pleased the Pharaoh to give this authority to Joseph.

And God said of man: "<u>let them have dominion ... over all the earth</u> ". And this pleases God.

In God giving man authority to rule the earth: Man became responsible for what has happened and is happening in the earth realm. God said: "<u>let them have dominion</u> ... <u>over all the earth</u>". When God spoke it, it became an irrevocable Law.

A number of books have been written in an effort to explain why God allows unjust occurrences to take place. The truth is it's man's responsibility. For when God said, "Let man have dominion over the earth", He placed the rule of earth in the hands of mankind.

It is not that God does not work upon the earth. But He only does so through a man of God, through His ambassadors. If He was to do it any other way He would be revoking His Law, and we know from His Word that is impossible.

Scripture, itself, testifies of this truth. **Hebrews 11:7 By faith Noah, being divinely warned of things not yet seen, moved with godly fear, prepared an ark for the saving of his household, by which he** *(Noah)* **condemned the world and became heir of the righteousness which is according to faith. (NKJ)**

God through Noah destroyed the rulers of the earth that was perverting the will of God. Their hearts housed evil continually producing corruption and bringing them under God's judgment. The flood was a result of man, therefore, making man accountable for it before God. As is man for the destruction in the world today, man has perverted what God made perfect.

The bible records that God continued to work throughout history using His ambassadors as the legal vessels in the earth. In destroying evildoers, God was preserving a remnant of people who would do His will on earth. Thank God that he upholds the righteous and makes them prosper.

When God heard the cry of His people in the land of Egypt He delivered them. The Bible says that He took them by the hand and led them out. The channel in which God chose to deliver them was through a man named Moses. A man that would speak God's will as an able ambassador. Moses was God's ambassador to the Jews.

NOTE: In the next two chapters we will be looking at the fact that even though man is a ruler and God has given him the earth to rule over, he does not possess a throne of his own. Man must operate under the authority of an established spiritual power. Just like Joseph had no throne of his own and derived his power, his authority, from the Pharaoh's throne, so mankind reigns from either the kingdom of Light or from the kingdom of darkness. Man has no power to reign independently.

Then came Jesus; the second Adam who would restore God's kingdom here on earth.

Now there are two levels of authority given to man.

1. The authority given to mankind through Adam.
2. The authority given to those who are in Christ Jesus, those who have been born of the Spirit of God.

Adam was the first born ruler over all the earth. **Genesis 1:26-27 Then God said, "Let Us make man in Our image, according to Our likeness; let them have dominion over the fish of the sea, over the birds of the air, and over the cattle, over <u>all</u> the earth and over every creeping thing that creeps on the earth." So God created man in His own image; in the image of God He created him; male and female He created them. (NKJ)**

BUT, Jesus is the first born over ALL God's creation, seen and unseen; because He is God and He is man.

> **Colossians 1:15-16 He** *(Jesus)* **is the image of the invisible God, the firstborn over <u>all creation.</u> For by Him all things were created that are in heaven and that are on earth, visible and invisible, whether thrones or dominions or principalities or powers. All things were created through Him and for Him. (NKJ)**

Can you see that mankind who chooses to enter into a covenant relationship with God, through faith in Jesus, has been elevated to an eminently higher level of authority? We have been given the privilege and responsibility of using the authority of God's Word; Jesus' authority. We have been called to the position of an ambassador of the living Word of God.

Matthew 28:18-20 And Jesus came and spoke to them, saying, "<u>All authority</u> has been given to Me in heaven and on earth. "Go therefore and make disciples of all the nations, baptizing them in the name of the Father and of the Son and of the Holy Spirit, "teaching them to observe all things that I have commanded you; and lo, I am with you always, even to the end of the age." Amen. (NKJ)

When Paul wrote to Titus he instructed him to use <u>all authority</u>. **[Titus 2:15]**. If we speak in accordance with the Word of God and hold fast to it, all power then is subject to us. Every principality and power, everything that has a name, must submit to the authority given to the ambassadors of God's Word.

Jesus came to do the will of His heavenly Father, creating a kingdom of ambassadors who will continue to further the will of their heavenly Father here on earth.

Isaiah 9:6-7 *(Speaking of Jesus)* **For unto us a Child is born, unto us a Son is**

given; and the government will be upon His shoulder. And His name will be called wonderful, Counselor, Mighty God, everlasting Father, Prince of Peace. Of the increase of His government and peace there will be no end, upon the throne of David and over His kingdom, to order it and establish it with judgment and justice from that time forward, even forever. The zeal of the LORD of hosts will perform this. (NKJ)

Revelation 1:5-6 ... To Him who loved us and washed us from our sins in His own blood, and has made us kings and priests to His God and Father, to Him be glory and dominion forever and ever. Amen. (NKJ)

Jesus has established through His blood covenant a new kingdom of kings to rule over His domain. And established priests for His God and Father, to Him be glory and dominion forever and ever. Amen.

As rulers in this Kingdom, our authority is far superior to those in any other kingdom. **Deuteronomy 32:30-31 How could one chase a thousand, and two put ten thousand to flight, unless their Rock had sold them, and the LORD had surrendered them? For their rock is not like our Rock, even our enemies themselves being judges. (NKJ)** If God be for us what can stand against us? The answer is nothing!

Jesus told parables concerning the kingdom of heaven and in those parables He made it very clear that we have been given dominion over His kingdom here on earth.

> **Luke 20:9 Then He began to tell the people this parable: "A certain man planted a vineyard, leased it to vinedressers, and went into a far country for a long time. (NKJ)**
>
> **Matt 25:14 "For the kingdom of heaven is like a man traveling to a far country, who called his own servants and delivered his goods to them. (NKJ)**
>
> **Mark 13:34 "It is like a man going to a far country, who left his house and gave authority to his servants, and to each his work, and commanded the doorkeeper to watch. (NKJ)**
>
> **Luke 19:12-13 Therefore He said: "A certain nobleman went into a far country to receive for himself a kingdom and to return. "So he called ten of his servants, delivered to them ten minas, and said to them, 'Do business till I come.' (NKJ)**

Who has gone away? Is it not Jesus? And who did he put in charge of his dominion? Is it not us, His body?

God did not create us and give us authority over His kingdom here on earth so that we could do our own thing; God's desire is for us to live a life of obedience to His Word through the power of His Spirit. And in so doing fulfill His will through our life.

Matthew 6:9-10 "In this manner, therefore, pray: our Father in heaven, hallowed be Your name. Your kingdom come. Your will be done on earth as it is in heaven. (NKJ)

What a privilege to be a part of God's kingdom, to have the opportunity to be His ambassador's to our families, our communities and the world. Remember it was at the high cost to Jesus that God established His kingdom of kings and priests here on earth. So let us never take our responsibility lightly. Let us sell out completely to the cause of Christ.

Concluding statement for this chapter: God created mankind to be in His likeness and image, that God might be seen in us and through us. Man is to be in the physical realm what God is in the spiritual realm. This is accomplished through man's intimate relationship with God. When man sinned and separated himself from God he no longer reflected the image of His Creator. God had to send His Son into the world in order that man may again be restored to the likeness of God. Through that act of redemption God has now placed His Spirit in us that we might once again reflect His image to all creation.

1. Man has been a ruler from his first breath. **[Genesis 1:26-28]**
2. God ordained that man would rule, it was not man's decision. **[Genesis 1:26-28]**
3. Because man has dominion over the earth when he became corrupted, he corrupted

his domain. **[Genesis 3:17 - Romans 5:16]**

4. Jesus restored the kingdom of God through His blood, and created a kingdom of kings and priests for His Father. **[Revelation 1:5-6]**
5. Because of the indwelling of the Holy Spirit we again reflect the image of our Creator God. **[1 Corinthians 15:49]**
6. Through our unity with Christ we have the power to bring all things in submission to the Word of God. **[Luke 10:19]**

Bring Glory to God! Use Jesus' authority to defeat every enemy that exalts itself against the Word of God!

CHAPTER FOUR

A HIGHER REALITY

Romans 8:37b ... we are more than conquerors through Him who loved us. (NKJ)

As "developed nations" we tend to be advanced in our capabilities and productivity because of our being educated. The name of our game is to educate. One of the definitions of educate is "to provide with information". This is a feeding of the mind. The mind loves to hear facts and figures so that it may reason. Because they have left out God, this has produced for the most part nothing more than a whole lot of intellectualism in the nations that are supposed to be so far advanced.

Your intellect cannot heal. It cannot set a demon-possessed individual free. It cannot raise the dead. No, our intellect will instead try to talk us out of this realm of the spirit on the basis of reason. The mind will say "This does not add up with the facts and figures I have been given". You see then how that the enemy has blinded the eyes of countless many to the spirit realm. And in doing so has rendered them powerless to deal with the circumstances of life that should be, can only be dealt with spiritually.

This deception could be likened to the Trojan Horse. The enemy strategically snuck into the heart of the great city Troy by way of the belly of a huge wooden horse. They were totally undetected for the simple fact that they were unseen. The enemy was right in their midst yet they did not realize it. As the city slept the enemy emerged from their wooden cover. The invading army overtook the city before they were able to defend themselves. Their city was destroyed, caught unaware.

Modern science based in their intellectual, educated views is one example of the Trojan Horse. Science has worked hard to deny the existence of the spirit realm; primarily denying that there is God. The result ... Many individuals, including those in the body of Christ, do not realize that the enemy is in their midst.

Nor do they understand that the spirit realm is far superior to the physical realm that can be detected by the five senses. The spirit realm is also far superior to the intellectual realm that can explain with reasoning.

To the individuals that are limited to the physical, intellectual realms, the spirit realm is relegated as being superstition or figments of our imaginations.

It only adds fuel to the fire when most "Christians" think that the spirit world is just something that we will deal with in the sweet by and by. But in the here and now; we just get by and then we die. Because of their ignorance in the Word of God concerning the spirit realm they have become victims of the unseen. For we have not detected the enemy in our midst. So; let us wake up and expose the enemy before our "city" is destroyed. Amen!

Our very existence and future depends entirely upon the spiritual realm. The foundation for the physical world we live in is established in the spiritual realm. If it were not for the spiritual realm there would be no physical realm.

In speaking to Job God asked: "Where were you when I laid the foundations of the earth? Tell Me, if you have understanding." **[Job 38:4]** This foundation according to **Hebrews 1:10** was laid by the Lord... **'"You, Lord, in the beginning laid the foundation of the earth, and the heavens are the work of Your hands."(NKJ)** Then **Hebrews 11:3** goes on to declare how things are made... **"By faith we understand that the worlds were framed by the word of God, so that the things which are seen were not made of things which are visible."(NKJ)** You see then that the foundation of the natural, physical realm was made from that which is unseen.... the spirit realm. The Word declares in **John 6:63b** that **"...The words that I speak to you are spirit, and they are life."(NKJ)** All that has been created then has been established upon the Word of God. God said, **"Let there be..."** and there was. No matter what you have been told, the fact is that all that was created was created by God's Words which are spirit.

MAN DID NOT CREATE THE SPIRIT WORLD, BUT THROUGH GOD, WHO IS SPIRIT WAS THE VISIBLE AND INVISIBLE WORLDS CREATED.

Colossians 1:15-17 He is the image of the invisible God, the firstborn over all creation. For by Him all things were created that are in heaven and that are on earth, visible and invisible, whether thrones or dominions or principalities or powers. All things were created through Him and for Him. And He is before all things, and in Him all things consist. (NKJ)

THEREFORE THE PHYSICAL REALM IS GOVERNED BY SPIRITUAL LAWS.

Man does not have the ability to create spiritual laws. These laws have already been set in motion by the Creator of all things. We live by these laws everyday, sometimes not even realizing that there in operation. For an example: your tongue. There is a spiritual law recorded in **Proverbs 18:21** which states: **"Death and life are in the power of the tongue, and those who love it will eat its fruit."(NKJ)** This spiritual law states that you have power in your tongue and in that death or life is released for you to partake of. This is only one of numerous spiritual laws.

Spiritual laws are like the law of gravity; you cannot see gravity but the law of gravity works every time. What goes up must come down when the law of gravity is working. You cannot see spoken words but they are either working for you or against you every day of your life. Have you ever said "I told you it would happen" or "Didn't I say that would happen". You see you are living in the power of the words that you have been speaking whether death or life.

The man who only relies on his physical strength or intellectual faculties is left weak and limited. But the person who knows and understands the spirit realm and its spiritual laws is a mighty force.

Note: Spiritual laws apply to the saved and unsaved alike.

The natural laws such as gravity, time, and space have no authority over spiritual laws, but spiritual laws do have power and authority over the natural, physical realm which includes natural laws, gravity, time, space, and so on. The truth of spiritual law superseding natural law is highly exhibited throughout Gods Word. Peter had the ability to walk "on" the water. Philip was translated from one place to another by the power of the Holy Spirit. The sick, throughout New Testament scriptures, are healed instantly. The dead were brought back to life. These are all contrary to natural, physical laws known to man, but are all accessible through faith in spiritual laws.

However, we must understand that spiritual laws also make it possible for a perfectly healthy individual to drop dead after being cursed. Remember, death and life is in the power of the tongue. Cursing is done with the tongue.

Those who speak curses are subjects of the kingdom of darkness. And the dark side is ruled by a fallen angel on an ego trip to take over the world. His desire is to steal, kill, and destroy. **[John 10:10]** Satan is his name and stealing, killing, and destroying is his game.

Witchcraft is one of his tactics to steal, kill, and destroy. Witchcraft is far greater than you may realize. I am not referring to witches intentionally placing spells on people, though they do exist. What we must realize is that the power of witchcraft is the power to take control of one's mind resulting in loss, destruction, or death. We are exposed to witchcraft in our schools, the media, the health care profession, family and many well meaning people. In some cases, even church leaders can be causing you to believe in ways that will result in loss, destruction, or premature death.

If our minds are controlled by anything other than the Word of God we are bewitched. Bewitched by definition is: To completely captivate someone; to take control through one's mind.

Gal 3:1-3 O foolish Galatians! Who has bewitched you that you should not obey the truth, before whose eyes Jesus Christ was clearly portrayed among you as crucified? This only I want to learn from you: Did you receive the Spirit by the works of the law, or by the hearing of faith? Are you so foolish? Having begun in the Spirit, are

you now being made perfect by the flesh? (NKJ)

This is not a flesh issue, this is a spiritual issue. We are not to be completely captivated by the flesh realm, by the intellect, by the enemy which will cause us to not obey the truth. God's Word is truth.

I am here to tell you we have all been bewitched in some way or another. This is why we are instructed to renew or renovate or reform our minds to what the word of God says. In doing so we break the power of those controlling, captivating "spells".

Ephesians 4:23 and be renewed in the spirit of your mind, And **Romans12:2 "And do not be conformed to this world, but be transformed by the renewing of your mind, that you may prove what is that good and acceptable and perfect will of God." (NKJ)** This word "transformed" means changing from one form into another like metamorphosis. Renewing or a renovating of the mind will discard the old thoughts that have been holding you in bondage, under the control of another. Being under the control of another is exactly what happens when a curse is placed. The individual under the curse is held in bondage to another in their thought realm. That is why as children of God we must be anchored in the Word of God so that we can not be taken captive.

Ask yourself: What thoughts are controlling my mind? Who are those thoughts coming from? Have I tested the thought according to God's Word? Am I seeing myself as mere man under the control of circumstance or am I seeing myself as I really am, a son or daughter of the Most High God, with authority and power to cause physical change?

Remember: The spirit realm is far superior to the natural, physical realm and curses have spiritual power.

We can hide our heads in the sand like an ostrich and deny that there is a spirit realm; however, our denying the spirit realm will in no way diminish the power of the spirit realm over the natural, physical realm. I said, denying the spirit realm in no way diminishes the power of the spirit realm over the physical! Our denial will only make us easy prey for the enemy, who by the way is in the spirit realm using spiritual laws against you in order to steal, kill, and destroy you.

Ephesians 6:12 For we do not wrestle against flesh and blood, but against principalities, against powers, against the rulers of the darkness of this age, against spiritual hosts of wickedness in the heavenly places. (NKJ)

It is to our advantage and I would say of a necessity that we understand the spirit realm and the spiritual laws that govern both in the spirit realm and in the physical realm. They effect and enable us to be all that we have been created in Christ Jesus to be. We have been created to rule and reign; as we abide by and enforce the spiritual laws of the kingdom of light, in which we live. Our King desires that His Father's will be done here on earth as it is in heaven. That we operate in His spiritual laws to benefit mankind and in doing so bring glory to Him.

We have been created by God to rule in His domain, and He elevated us to that position through His Son Jesus. The devil's position, however, is to try to pull you down from your position of rule through deception, ignorance, or lack of revelation in the Word of God.

Ephesians 2:4-6 But God, who is rich in mercy, because of His great love with which He loved us, even when we were dead in trespasses, made us alive together with Christ (by grace you have been saved), and raised us up together, and made us sit together in the heavenly places in Christ Jesus, (NKJ)

Christ Jesus is sitting on the throne that is above all other principalities and powers and we are seated with Him. This obviously is positional not literal. Our position is that of power and authority which is far above any other power or authority or throne in the spirit realm. We rule with authority and power when we are operating in the revelation that we are seated in His authority. This is the authority of Jesus... the same authority that was the Word that became flesh and dwelt among us and defeated the enemy making an open show of him. So this overcoming power and authority is released through faith in the Word of God.

John 15:5 "'I am the vine, you are the branches. He who abides in Me, and I in him, bears much fruit; for without Me you can do nothing." (NKJ)

We need to know God's laws; His Word, that governs supreme so that we might be effective rulers in Christ Jesus. When we are trained in the laws governing the spiritual realm the effect will be manifested in the physical realm. This will be evident in our authority over all principalities and powers that have exalted themselves against or above the Word of God.

John 14:12-14 "Most assuredly, I say to you, he who believes in Me, the works that I do he will do also; and greater works than these he will do, because I go to My Father. "And whatever you ask in My name, that I will do, that the Father may be glorified in the Son. "If you ask anything in My name, I will do it. (NKJ)

Now we know that Jesus is the Word of God so let me paraphrase **[John 14:12-14]**

"Most assuredly, I say to you, he who believes in the Word of God and its authority, the works that I do he will do also; and greater works than these he will do, because I go to My Father. "And whatever you ask in accordance with the authority of the Word, that I will do, that the Father may be glorified in the

Son. "If you ask anything according to <u>the Word</u>, I will do it.

Don't ask God to change your neighbor into a cow because He backed over your trash can. The Word does not give you authority to ask for that. But you can ask for grace to forgive him.

Again, Jesus is our example: When Jesus was confronted by the devil, He said: **"It is written ..."** **[Luke 4:4]**. When Jesus said: "It is written" He was saying: It has been established in heaven.

When we are dealing with a devil that has exalted, or is trying to exalt itself in opposition to the Word of God we are to declare what is written with faith in the authority of the Word of God to bring it to pass. God's word is the law.

Isaiah 55:11 So shall My word be that goes forth from My mouth; it shall not return to Me void, but it shall accomplish what I please, and it shall prosper in the thing for which I sent it. (NKJ)

In the spirit realm the Word of God has been placed far above all other principalities and powers.

We can shout and scream at the devil until we are red in the face and it will not detour the demon. But if we whisper the Word of God in faith, the demon must submit to the Word. For the throne of Jesus is over ALL principalities and powers, physical or spiritual. God's kingdom has ample power in which to enforce the Word spoken.

When we exercise faith in what is available to us in the spiritual realm, such as God's Word and His Spirit, we can overcome natural obstacles that we face in this life. This is what Jesus was telling us in **Mark 11:22-24 So Jesus answered and said to them, "Have faith in God. "For assuredly, I say to you, whoever says to this mountain, 'Be removed and be cast into the sea,' and does not doubt in his heart, but believes that those things he says will come to pass, he will have whatever he says. "Therefore I say to you, whatever things you ask when you pray, believe that you receive them, and you will have them. (NKJ)**

That is a spiritual law that supersedes the natural law, and like all God's laws it is designed to benefit us. BUT we need to put our faith in His Word to activate the promises, for without faith there is no activation.

NOTE: If we will put our faith in God's Word, our faith can move us out of the natural realm, the world's system, and into the spiritual realm, often referred to as the supernatural. And God's desire is that we would rely upon His supernatural power.

Man was created to operate in the supernatural power of God; to govern the natural world by it. And our source to that supernatural power is our faith in the Word of God.

I John 5:4 For whatever is born of God overcomes the world. And this is the victory that has overcome the world—our faith. (NKJ)

Let me explain briefly the power of faith. In **Hebrews 11:1** it says: **"Now faith is the substance of things hoped for, the evidence of things not seen." (NKJ)**

When the Lord compelled me to study faith He took me to Hebrews 11:1. He then instructed me to observe the dictionary definition of SUBSTANCE. The Webster's Ninth New Collegiate Dictionary defines it as the: "ultimate reality that underlies all outward manifestations and change". Now; applying this definition to Hebrews 11:1; we see that our faith is the ultimate reality that underlies all outward manifestations and change. And the substance of our faith is God's Word. For when our faith is connected to God's Word we are connected to the throne of God and His supreme power.

Let's take this revelation even farther as we apply this definition of faith to the account of Peter walking on the water. **Matthew 14:28-31 And Peter answered Him and said, "Lord, if it is You, command me to come to You on the water." So He said, "Come." And when Peter had come down out of the boat, he walked on the water to go to Jesus. But when he saw that the wind was boisterous, he was afraid; and beginning to sink he cried out, saying, "Lord, save me!" And immediately Jesus stretched out His hand and caught him, and said to him, "O you of little faith, why did you doubt?" (NKJ)**

Peter's faith in Jesus' word "come" created a reality that for him had never before existed. But when fear overtook Peter's faith, his new reality was destroyed and he found himself once again under the rule of the natural law causing him to sink. As Peter focused on the Giver of the word "come" he no longer was limited by natural laws but was experiencing the benefits of the supernatural. However, when his focus was given to the natural realm fear entered, nullifying his faith, subsequently destroying his ability to operate in the supernatural.

What can we, as believers, learn from this account? The same as Peter we must focus our hearts and minds on Jesus, not allowing the circumstances that arise in the natural realm to distract us from the Word.

Remember: If we are to create a supernatural reality and maintain it we must believe and not doubt.

Can you conceive going beyond the natural realm into the supernatural to create new realities through faith in the Word of God?

Jesus who is the Word said in **John 16:33b "... In the world you will have tribulation; but be of good cheer, I have overcome the world." (NKJ)**

Victory over the world is attainable ONLY through faith in the Word of God. Human strength and abilities, mental training and endurance, or any other natural exertion will never accomplish what can only be done through faith in the Word.

Are you operating in victory? If not, what is holding you down? Is it that you need a new reality? In the Word of God you will find the authority to change your reality: JUST BELIEVE.

Mark 9:23 Jesus said to him, "If you can believe, all things are possible to him who believes." (NKJ) Do you believe that the Word has authority above and beyond your present reality? I can assure you that it does! However your belief in that Word is absolutely essential in changing your present reality. Scripture declares "as a man believes in his heart so is he". And Jesus also said: "In accordance with your faith be it done onto you."

On the other hand fear can do the same thing. You can say about the mountain that is in your way: "I am afraid that this mountain is getting bigger and bigger", and if you do not doubt in your heart, but believe what you say, it will come to pass. Unfortunately, this is the way many Christians are talking. They are being overcome and not overcoming according to the supernatural power available to them through faith in the Word of God.

Fear has the ability to create realities in our lives also. And Satan is more than willing to bring about any negative reality that we will believe. So be careful what you believe, and say!

Proverb 10:24 The fear of the wicked will come upon him, and the desire of the righteous will be granted. (NKJ)

As you conclude this chapter I urge you to make a commitment to yourself; that you will give yourself regularly to the study and meditation of God's supernatural law. Laws that will create realities for us that are beyond the natural realm; if we will just take God at His word. Let us never forget the importance of knowing, and relying upon those laws to overcome every thought or pretense that will try to exalt itself against God's Word.

The physical realm and the spirit realm are two distinct realms, yet they are one and cannot be separated. To operate from the physical realm mind set limits us considerable. God's desire is that we operate out of a spiritual mind set so that we might be effective ambassadors of the kingdom of God here on earth.

1 Corinthians 3:1-3 And I, brethren, could not speak to you as to spiritual people but as to carnal, as to babes in Christ. I fed you with milk and not with solid food; for until now you were not able to receive it, and even now you are still not able; for you are still carnal. For where there are envy, strife, and divisions among you, are you not carnal and behaving like mere men? (NKJ)

Are we now ready for solid food?

1. The spirit realm is far superior to the physical realm that we experience with our senses. **[Luke 10:19]**
2. By God who is spirit was the physical worlds created. **[Genesis 1]**

3. Natural laws are subject to spiritual laws, but spiritual laws are not subject to natural laws. **[Matthew 14:28-31]**

4. Faith in God's Word which is spirit will give us the victory over the tribulation that we face in this world. **[John 16:33]**

Let us put our faith in the Word of God to create a supernatural reality as we reflect Jesus to a needy and hurting world.

Bring Glory to God by using Jesus' authority to defeat every enemy that exalts itself against the Word of God!

CHAPTER FIVE

TWO KINGDOMS

John 3:19-21 "And this is the condemnation, that the light has come into the world, and men loved darkness rather than light, because their deeds were evil. "For everyone practicing evil hates the light and does not come to the light, lest his deeds should be exposed. "But he who does the truth comes to the light, that his deeds may be clearly seen, that they have been done in God." (NKJ)

Two kingdoms; they are the kingdom of light versus the kingdom of darkness. Regardless of whether we like it or not, the truth of the matter is that all humanity is producing fruit for one or the other kingdom. There is no neutral ground.

Of these two kingdoms the first and highly superior one is the kingdom of light. That throne belongs to God our Creator. The laws that govern in His kingdom are just and true, filled with mercy and grace.

Who is a part of God's kingdom? Only those that are one with God. And that only happens through submitting to, and abiding in the Word of God. Only those who have the Spirit of God can abide in the Word, for God's Word is spirit. Therefore it can only be understood by those who have been made spiritually alive through rebirth. **[John 6:63 & 1 Corinthians. 2:13-14]**

John 15:7 "If you abide in Me, and My words abide in you, you will ask what you desire, and it shall be done for you. (NKJ)

When we abide in the Word we are abiding in the spiritual realm; in God's kingdom. Outside of His Word we do not have citizenship in the kingdom of God.

John 14:6 Jesus said to him, "I am the way, the truth, and the life. No one comes to the Father except through Me. (NKJ) The only way to the Father is through faith in the living Word of God. **[John 1:1-14]**

As the Word declares, abiding is the key that unlocks God's kingdom in us and through us. To know about God will not unlock the kingdom of God for us. But to know God through abiding in His living Word most assuredly unlocks the kingdom for us.

God's Word is His covenant for us **[Isaiah 43]**. And if we are to overcome the darkness in this world we must be covenant members of the kingdom of

Light. We have been made one with the light through our abiding in the Word. Us serving God's kingdom and God's kingdom serving us.

The second kingdom which is acutely inferior to the first kingdom is the kingdom of darkness. That throne belongs to Satan, a fallen chief angel who tried to overthrow God in heaven resulting in his downfall.

The main objective of Satan's kingdom is to discredit God's Word among men. Oh how Satan loves to use his lies to take captive those who are deceived, then he uses them to advocate his deceptions producing evil among men.

In the process of Satan's rebellion, he did take one-third of the angels with him and they are the demonic spirits that we must war against as we establish the kingdom of heaven on earth.

Mankind who rebels against God's laws has no choice but to live under and to promote Satan's destruction. They will by nature speak in opposition to God's Word, speaking lies on Satan's behalf. And because Satan's kingdom is a spiritual kingdom it does have power over the physical realm. Satan exercises his authority as he uses God's spiritual laws to bring destruction. Such as: "As a man believes in his heart so is he." The devil knows God's Word and knows how to use it against us. That is what he did with Eve and that is what he tried to do with Jesus.

Satan's passion is to get us to believe that we are less than what God says we are. If we will agree with his words we become what the devil said we are. It is the law "As a man believes in his heart so is he."

That is just an example of how Satan uses God's laws against us. He is our accuser; and the only way we can overcome him is through faith in the blood of the Lamb and the word of our testimony.

Satan was a chief angel with much authority enabling him to get one third of the angels to rebel with him. Now whether one third of the angels were what Satan had authority over in heaven I do not know. This I do know, He still has much authority, too much for man to deal with in his own authority.

Jude 1:9 Yet Michael the archangel, in contending with the devil, when he disputed about the body of Moses, dared not bring against him a reviling accusation, but said, "The Lord rebuke you!" (NKJ)

When we must deal with demons *(lying spirits)* it must be in the name of the Lord and not flippantly. We must stick to the authority of the Word. If we do not have the Word backing us we will be void of any authority over the demonic. We will find ourselves out on a limb and the demon cutting it off.

Gal 6:1 Brethren, if a man is overtaken in any trespass, you who are spiritual restore such a one in a spirit of gentleness, considering yourself lest you also be tempted. (NKJ) We must stay on our guard against the work of the devil.

I did say, and reiterate that God's kingdom is far superior to Satan's. But it would be dangerous for us to under estimate Satan's power. To do so we would be unprepared to do battle against him. Only the Word of God spoken by Jesus' ambassadors can render Satan powerless.

I am not here to glorify Satan and his kingdom by talking about him. What I am here to do is expose him to the light. It is the light that renders him defenseless; but for those in darkness he remains king.

DECEIT IS THE DEVIL'S RIGHT ARM!

In John 8:44 Jesus said of those who were opposing Him. "You are of your father the devil, and the desires of your father you want to do. He was a murderer from the beginning, and does not stand in the truth, because there is no truth in him. When he speaks a lie, he speaks from his own resources, for he is a liar and the father of it. (NKJ)

Satan only has power in one realm and that is in darkness. Darkness refers to the lack of truth. And where there is a lack of truth Satan reigns.

There are those who walk in darkness out of the lack of knowledge of the truth and others out of a willful desire to do so. In either case they are under Satan's rule, part of his kingdom, and subject to his deceptions.

Only truth can set us free, delivering us out of the power of darkness. **John 8:31-36 Then Jesus said to those Jews who believed Him, "If you <u>abide</u> in My word, you are My disciples indeed. "And you shall know the truth, and the truth shall make you**

free." They answered Him, "We are Abraham's descendants, and have never been in bondage to anyone. How can you say, 'You will be made free'?" Jesus answered them, "Most assuredly, I say to you, whoever commits sin is a slave of sin. "And a slave does not abide in the house forever, but a son abides forever. "Therefore if the Son makes you free, you shall be free indeed. (NKJ)

Two kingdoms; who are diametrically opposed to each other, they are as different as light and dark. These kingdoms are continuously at war with each other, for there can be no common ground between these two spiritual kingdoms. For when light comes in contact with darkness, darkness is destroyed, they cannot coexist. The battle goes on and the battle front is man's domain. Who will control it? Can Satan keep mankind in darkness or will the light of God over take the darkness through Christ's ambassadors? The final outcome has been predetermined, God's kingdom wins. We know that because God's Word declares it and God's Word cannot be altered. But we are still called to the battle, called to shine forth in Jesus' name.

It is written in **Ephesians 6:12 "For we do not wrestle against flesh and blood, but against principalities, against powers, against the rulers of the darkness of this age, against spiritual hosts of wickedness in the heavenly places." (NKJ)**

What are: ... "spiritual hosts of wickedness in the heavenly places."? To put it in a nutshell, they are well established lies that are accepted as truth by the rulers of this earth. They are designed by their nature to keep us from the truth. They are lies that have been exalted by mankind higher than God's Word allowing them to rule upon this earth. This is what we are wrestling against, those things that have exalted itself above God's Word.

Remember: We can only do battle if we know the truth and live in the truth.

2 Corinthians 10:4-6 For the weapons of our warfare are not carnal but mighty in God for pulling down strongholds, casting down arguments and every high thing that exalts itself against the knowledge of God, bringing every thought into captivity to the obedience of Christ, and being ready to punish all disobedience when your obedience is fulfilled. (NKJ)

As members of God's kingdom, through becoming one with the Word, we are not to give ground to Satan. We are not to allow the darkness to overtake us, but instead we are to take ground that Satan has been holding. We are to do so by shedding light upon the darkness that is in this world. In Jesus' Name we shall!

Again, God's throne is far superior to Satan's throne and in due time, God's time, the light will totally defeat Satan, and he will be locked up in hell, paying the price for his rebellion against God almighty. He then will never again be able to pervert God's will, His good, pleasing, perfect will. What a day that will be, when there will be nothing opposing the Word of God.

BUT in the mean time, Jesus' ambassadors must continue the battle against these evil forces, these lying spirits. To do so we need to know and understand not only our enemy, we also need to know the power of the kingdom of God which we are a part of through the abiding Word that is written upon our heart by the Spirit of God.

Ezekiel 36:26-27 "I will give you a new heart and put a new spirit within you; I will take the heart of stone out of your flesh and give you a heart of flesh. "I will put My Spirit within you and cause you to walk in My statutes, and you will keep My judgments and do them. (NKJ)

I want to stop here to elaborate further on what it means to abide in the Word. In **[John 1:1-4]** it explains to us that Jesus is the eternal Word and in **[John 1:14** it says that the Word became flesh and dwelt among us. And **Rev 19:13** says: **"He was clothed with a robe dipped in blood, and His name is called The Word of God." (NKJ)** So we must always keep in mind when we read about Jesus, it is speaking of the living Word of God. So when Jesus said: **John 14:6 "I am the way and the truth and the life. No one comes to the Father except through me."(NKJ)** Jesus was telling us that the only way to the Father and eternal life is through the Word, which is truth. It is not a truth but THE TRUTH.

And in John 15:5-6 Jesus said, **"I am the vine; you are the branches. If a man remains in me and I in him, he will bear much fruit; apart from me you can do nothing. If anyone does not remain in me, he is like a branch that is thrown away and withers; such branches are picked up, thrown into the fire and burned." (NKJ)**

Now let me paraphrase that: The <u>Word</u>, the <u>Truth</u>, is the vine that connects us to God. If a man remains in the <u>Truth</u> and the <u>Truth</u> remains in him, he will bear much fruit; apart from the <u>Truth</u> you can do nothing for the kingdom of <u>light</u>. If anyone does not remain in the <u>Truth</u>, he is like a branch that is thrown away and withers; such branches are picked up, thrown into the fire and burned.

Abiding in the Word means that we are living our life in such a way that it reflects the Word that is in us, this is done through the abiding presence of the Holy Spirit who makes the Word a reality in us. If there be anything in us that is not in agreement with the Word we are to cast it down, so that God's Word will reign through us to God's glory. When we do so we are ready to take our place with Christ, the exalted Word reigning over the darkness in this world until all God's enemies, all lies that has exalted itself against God's Word, is made His footstool.

2 Corinthians 4:6-7 For it is the God who commanded light to shine out of darkness, who has shone in our hearts to give the light of the knowledge of the glory of God in the face of Jesus Christ. But we have this

treasure in earthen vessels, that the excellence of the power may be of God and not of us. (NKJ)

We are the earthen vessels that have been filled with the knowledge of the Word and the power of the Holy Spirit to be the light of the world, for God's glory. A light bulb is of no effect in itself, but when there is power present it is that instrument of light that will eliminate the darkness.

Matt 5:14-16 "You are the light of the world. A city that is set on a hill cannot be hidden. "Nor do they light a lamp and put it under a basket, but on a lampstand, and it gives light to all who are in the house. "Let your light so shine before men, that they may see your good works and glorify your Father in heaven. (NKJ)

Let me list just a few things that stand opposed to God's Word; sickness, disease, poverty, dying young, and so on. We are called to defeat these enemies by fully trusting in the Word of God. **Ps 103:1-5 Bless the LORD, O my soul; and all that is within me, bless His holy name! Bless the LORD, O my soul, and forget not all His benefits: Who forgives all your iniquities, who heals all your diseases, Who redeems your life from destruction, who crowns you with lovingkindness and tender mercies, Who satisfies your mouth with good things, so that**

your youth is renewed like the eagle's. (NKJ) May God's word be a reality in and through us.

Note: The power of the Word must be evident in our life before we can be light to others.

Ps 107:20 He sent His word and healed them, and delivered them from their destruction's. (NKJ)

Light always overcomes darkness and truth always rules over lies.

For example: If we had been led to believe a lie and some good fellow came along showing us the truth and we accepted the truth because we recognized it as truth, we would no longer be under the power of that lie.

On the other hand if we know what the truth is and some misguided fellow came alone and told us a lie, something contrary to the truth, we would not be mislead because we have known the truth. As light overcomes darkness, and darkness has no authority over light; so it is with truth, truth has the power to reign supreme over lies.

Take the teaching of evolution as an example: There are many who have been mislead by the lies of evolution. For the most part it is because they have never been exposed to the truth. Most rational thinking people when exposed to the truth of creation accepts the truth seeing evolution for what it is; a lie, an attempt by Satan to discredit God's Word and authority, and many have bought into his lies.

Where truth has been established no lie can overcome it, but where a lie has been established the truth has the power to destroy it. So if anyone chooses to live in darkness after being exposed to the truth; that is a willful act of disobedience against the truth.

In the absences of truth is fertile ground where a lie can prosper. That is why it is so important for us to be ready and willing to combat the lies of Satan with the truth. But we know that not everyone will accept the truth. Jesus said: **"... men loved darkness rather than light, because their deeds were evil." John 3:19b (NKJ)**

Jesus said of Satan that he is the father of all lies; that when Satan opens his mouth and speaks out come lies.

Man may think they are the ones who came up with these evolutionary theories, but it was Satan who planted those ideas in their minds. Satan knew that they would deceive many, while striking a strong blow against the Word of God. Satan is the father of all lies, not man; man is just the facilitator of his lies.

Satan's power is his ability to use lies to deceive, to cast doubt upon God's Word, tempting us to go against what God has said. And if we do not have a strong desire for the truth we too can be tempted to go against the truth.

Do you want to be above and not beneath? Then abide in the truth, for those who overcome abide in the truth; they refuse to let go of God's Word until it completes its work. **[Hebrews. 6:12]**

Are you gaining understanding into how Satan has been able to use mankind and their God given authority to corrupt this world? Man is the only one who can effect change upon this planet, per God's order. So in order for Satan to pervert what God made perfect, he must do so through man.

Which brings us to this spiritual law: Jesus said: **Matt 9:29 ... "According to your faith let it be to you." (NKJ)**

In direct response to what we believe we will receive, good or evil.

So in order for Satan to accomplish his will on earth he must get man to believe, trust in fully, his lies. NOTE: the more people who believe Satan's lie the more power that lie has to bear fruit. So do not follow blindly; always seek the truth. The Bible says: Those who seek find.

Have you exalted the Word of God above all other reports? The answer will be evident in what comes out of your mouth, for our mouth is the evidence of what we believe in our heart. It is from the fruit of our lips we shall eat.

These are spiritual laws that govern man, affecting all that man has authority over. And the natural man's authority is over ALL the earth.

For the man who has entered into a covenant relationship with God through faith in Jesus, that man's authority has been increased greatly to that of Jesus, He being the first born over all that God has created, seen and unseen. **[Col. 1:15]** So we have even a greater responsibility to guard our heart against Satan's deceptions; that we might not speak contrary to the Word of God.

If Satan can get man to believe his lies he will pass them on; we speak what we believe. In so doing he will activate Satan's lies by saying things that goes against what God has said. Remember how that worked among the Israelites when the spies came back from the Promised Land? Ten of them spread an evil report; an evil report is anything that goes against what God said. That evil report spread throughout the camp until it was believed by most everyone there.

Ten men swayed a million away from believing what God said. How were they able to do that? By getting the people to focus on the natural, like they had, in so doing they placed what can be seen above what God said. They rebelled against God's Word and gave into the spiritual power of fear. That evil report became more powerful to them than God's Word.

Have you determined in your heart to stand on God's Word regardless of what can be seen? We must or we will be prey for Satan's deception.

If God says that we can, but we say that we cannot, we are calling God a liar. And God will give us over to the reality of that lie, it is a spiritual law that cannot be broken, "As you believe so shall you receive."

Romans 3:3-4 For what if some did not believe? Will their unbelief make the faithfulness of God without effect? Certainly not! Indeed, let God be true but every man

a liar. As it is written: "That You may be justified in Your words, and may overcome when You are judged." (NKJ)

Do you always want to be right in what you say? Then let your speech be in agreement with the Word of God, regardless of what can be seen in the natural.

God's Word produces faith in those who will accept it, as they fully trust His Word. The results of trusting God's Word is that you will receive through faith and patience what God has promised, this is the fruit of faith in God's Word.

Do not be deceived by the candy coating that the devil hides his destructive perversion in. If the devil is offering you something that is appealing to you; and it will be appealing for he knows how to tempt us, know this that under that appealing coating is a center full of destruction.

STAY IN THE LIGHT; DON'T BE LURED INTO THE DARKNESS!

The world has become one with Satan and this is evident in all the destruction we see in the world today. There is sickness and disease and all sorts of perversions that affect this earth and its inhabitants.

Just listen to the advertisements that are so prevalent on TV. Such as; High cholesterol is something that you have no control over outside of medication, and it leads to heart attacks and strokes. Or one out of ten people have circulation problems in their legs, and the evil reports go on and on. All you have to do is start believing these reports and you to can have them.

But the Word of God says: **Exodus 23:25 "So you shall serve the LORD your God, and He will bless your bread and your water. And I will take sickness away from the midst of you. (NKJ)** The word translated sickness means disease, infirmities and sickness.

And again in **Ps 103:2-3 Bless the LORD, O my soul, and forget not all His benefits: Who forgives all your iniquities, who heals all your diseases, (NKJ)**

The question that is continually asked of us is: Who are you going to believe? It is easy to say when all is going well, "I'll believe the Word of God", but what happens when we hear an evil report, like the Israelites did? "If we go into that land we will be destroyed because the inhabitants there are much stronger than us." OR maybe you have received a report similar to this, "You have a disease that is going to kill you." *(There are giants in the land.)*

Will you surrender to fear accepting the evil report? Know that it is an evil report because it goes against what God has said. Or will you do like the two spies who came back with a good report, holding in confidence what God had said, believing that God was bigger than any enemy that they would face? They placed God's Word above what can be seen in the natural realm and receive what was promised. Will you?

2 Corinthians 5:7 For we walk by faith, not by sight. (NKJ) That implies that we walk by faith in God's Word and not by what the physical realm is telling us.

The ten spies that gave the evil report told what they seen, but what they failed to do was to trust God to fulfill His Word. REMEMBER the spiritual laws of God supersede the natural laws, those things that can be seen, that is IF we will remain in faith. God has commanded us over and over to "fear not" then we will see the might of the Lord.

As **Hebrews 10:38-39** states: **"Now the just shall live by faith; but if anyone draws back, my soul has no pleasure in him." But we are not of those who draw back to perdition, but of those who believe to the saving of the soul." (NKJ)**

The Israelites had no problem trusting God when all was going well, but when their life seemed to be in jeopardy they let fear reign; they failed to keep their trust in what God had promised.

The results of believing the evil report was that they did not receive what God had promised. God had promised and would have been faithful in performing it had they trusted Him, but their lack of faith exempted them from God's promises. It is by faith and patience that we receive the promises of God, there is NO other way. **[Hebrews 6:12]**

If you are not trusting God's Word you cannot enter into the land, the realm of God's promises. The only way into the land of promise was and is through faith in what God said.

Faith in God's Word produces health: **Ps 107:20 He sent His word and healed them, and delivered them from their destructions. (NKJ)**

As covenant people everything we need and desire in the Lord we can receive through faith in God's Word. Therefore don't let Satan rob you by surrendering your faith to fear that has been produced by what can be seen. God's Word is spirit and is superior to any physical or spiritual enemy that we might face.

Ps 37:4-5 Delight yourself also in the LORD, and He shall give you the desires of your heart. Commit your way to the LORD, trust also in Him, and He shall bring it to pass. (NKJ)

Paraphrased: Delight yourself also in the WORD, and He shall give you the desires of your heart. Commit your way to the WORD, trusting in the Word He shall bring it to pass.

Question: Will you trust your life to God's Word? Do we believe the Spiritual realm has more authority than the physical realm? What is stronger; your faith in God's Word or your fear as a result of an evil report?

So what if the Doctor told you that you had a disease that is killing you, but you knew what **1 Pet 2:24** said: *(Jesus)* **Himself bore our sins in His own body on the tree, that we, having died to sins, might live for righteousness—by whose stripes you were healed.(NKJ)** Or **Ps 103:1-3 Bless the**

LORD, O my soul; and all that is within me, bless His holy name! Bless the LORD, O my soul, and forget not <u>all</u> His benefits: Who forgives <u>all</u> your iniquities, who heals <u>all</u> your diseases, (NKJ)

I looked up to see what the word translated <u>all</u> means: It is translated from the Hebrew word **kol** and it means; ALL, the whole.

- Know **all** His benefits through faith in God's Word.
- Know He forgives **all** your iniquities, sins, through faith in God's Word.
- Know He heals **all** your diseases through faith in God's Word.

To know is not head knowledge, but heart knowledge, and faith is a fruit of the heart not the head. The Word comes in through our minds but then it must be written upon our hearts. **Hebrews 8:10 ... I will put My laws in their mind and write them on their hearts; and I will be their God, and they shall be My people. (NKJ)**

Faith comes from the truth and fear comes from the darkness. The battles go on; the outcome is up to you. Do you believe your God is bigger than your enemy? And that He stands behind His word?

The devil might say; "Yes you have got this disease; but just look at what the doctors can do for you; just put your trust in them." If the devil can get you to focus on what man can do for you, he can destroy you. Because your focus and trust is not in what God said, and God will not take second place to anything. I am not saying not to go to doctors; what I am saying is that if the doctor is the focus of your faith you are in trouble.

Jeremiah 17:5-8 Thus says the LORD: "Cursed is the man who trusts in man and makes flesh his strength, whose heart departs from the LORD. For he shall be like a shrub in the desert, and shall not see when good comes, but shall inhabit the parched places in the wilderness, in a salt land which is not inhabited. "Blessed is the man who trusts in the LORD, and whose hope is the LORD. For he shall be like a tree planted by the waters, which spreads out its roots by the river, and will not fear when heat comes; but its leaf will be green, and will not be anxious in the year of drought, nor will cease from yielding fruit. (NKJ)

Here are two examples which demonstrate the advantage of trusting in God over man. One king trusted in man and the other king sought the Lord.

2 Chronicles 16:12-13 And in the thirty-ninth year of his reign, Asa became diseased in his feet, and his malady was severe; yet in his disease he did not seek the LORD, but the physicians. So Asa rested with his fathers; he died in the forty-first year of his reign. (NKJ)

II Kings 20:1-6 In those days Hezekiah was sick and near death. And Isaiah the prophet, the son of Amoz, went to him and said to him, "Thus says the LORD: 'Set your house in order, for you shall die, and not live.'" Then he turned his face toward the wall, and prayed to the LORD, saying, "Remember now, O LORD, I pray, how I have walked before You in truth and with a loyal heart, and have done what was good in Your sight." And Hezekiah wept bitterly. And it happened, before Isaiah had gone out into the middle court, that the word of the LORD came to him, saying, "Return and tell Hezekiah the leader of My people, 'Thus says the LORD, the God of David your father: "I have heard your prayer, I have seen your tears; surely I will heal you. On the third day you shall go up to the house of the LORD. "And I will add to your days fifteen years. I will deliver you and this city from the hand of the king of Assyria; and I will defend this city for My own sake, and for the sake of My servant David."'" (NKJ)

Where do you turn in times of trouble? God wants us turning to Him, putting our faith in what he has promised; He alone has the power to deliver us from all our enemies. And He has said: **Exodus 15:26 .... For I am the LORD who heals you." (NKJ)**

The prophets have declared that God is our healer over and over again. The question is: "Do we believe that we were healed by His stripes or will we accept the evil report?"

What can be seen must remain a lesser reality than what God has said. Our faith is the evidence that we have what God said, not what we see in the natural. It is through faith and patience that we change our reality. Faith is not faith unless it is connected to patience.

Disciples of Jesus are not to be moved by what they see, but we are to be moved by what the Word of God says. Amen.

When we get to the end of it all, we do see that bad things do overpower people, even God's own precious children. We must ask the question: "Why"? It is because; What ever report we accept we will eat the fruit of that report, whether it is a good report or an evil one. Remember what Jesus said: "As you believe so shall you receive." And it is through Him that the spiritual laws are established. In that law is both, life and death; health and sickness, prosperity and lack, the outcome is in what you believe. Will it be God's Word that brings life and it more abundantly or the world's view of truth that will bring lack? Satan is the god of this world system, king of sickness, lack and poverty, so don't submit to his lordship.

What you have comes from what you believed. And to often our beliefs have been birth in ignorance of the Word. That ignorance can be, and is to often deadly!

Hosea 4:6a My people are destroyed for lack of knowledge. (NKJ)

We have got to wise up and stop blaming God for what we have created through our lack of faith and ignorance of God's Word. How easy it is for someone to get us to believe a lie if we do not have the truth established in our heart. If we are not abiding in the Word of God the devil will be planting his words in us, once they take root in us their fruit will be destructive for sure. Satan comes ONLY to kill, steal and destroy, never to bless, though it might look like it in the beginning.

Here is an evil report most people believe, taught to us by the world. That when you get old; your body becomes diseased; you get sick and die.

That is an evil report and it is from the devil, not God. But because most people believe that report and have surrendered to that reality, most people die that way. Those who are of the world must submit to those laws for they have no other reality. Not so for us who are of the kingdom of God, for God's Word should be our reality through faith. Amen.

Exodus 23:24-26 *God said:* **"You shall not bow down to their gods, nor serve them, nor do according to their works; but you shall utterly overthrow them and completely break down their sacred pillars. "So you shall serve the LORD your God, and He will bless your bread and your water. And I will take <u>sickness</u> away from the midst**

of you. "No one shall suffer miscarriage or be barren in your land; I will fulfill the number of your days. (NKJ)

Again; the word translated <u>sickness</u> is the Hebrew word: machaleh it means: disease, infirmity, sickness.

To paraphrase: If you are living in a right relationship with God through fully trusting in His word, He will take disease, infirmities, and sickness away from you. He did not say; I will take disease, infirmities, and sickness away from you until you are seventy or eighty or a hundred and then you will get diseased, become sick and die. In our natural thinking, that is thinking like the world thinks, we say how else will we die? How about like Moses a man who took God at His Word?

Deuteronomy 34:7 Moses was one hundred and twenty years old when he died. His eyes were not dim nor his natural vigor diminished. (NKJ) Moses was righteous in God's sight because he took God at His Word. And God considers us righteous in His sight when we believe in and trust fully in the living Word of God.

Moses, the man who received the Word from God that is written in [**Exodus 23:24-26**], believing God, he lived one hundred and twenty years. God's Word was manifested through Moses' faith as he lived in full strength to the day he died. Moses had no disease, infirmities, or sickness in his body up to his last breath on earth. God is no respecter of persons, so if He did it for Moses He will do it for all those who trust in His Covenant.

Acts 10:34 Then Peter opened his mouth and said: "In truth I perceive that God shows no partiality. (NKJ)

The good news is: **For all the promises of God in Him** (Jesus) **are Yes, and in Him Amen, to the glory of God through us. 2 Corinthians 1:20 (NKJ)** As God's promises worked for Moses so will they work for us through faith.

There were other Israelites at that time who were also God's covenant people who would not take God at His Word. They could not comprehend how faith in God's Word could affect the physical realm so they died prematurely in the desert, many from disease.

Do you know how to tell if the report you hear is a good report or an evil one, whether it comes from the kingdom of light or the kingdom of darkness? We can tell by using what we learn from **John 10:10 "The thief** *(Satan)* **does not come except to steal, and to kill, and to destroy. I** *(Jesus)* **have come that they may have life, and that they may have it more abundantly. (NKJ)**

John 10:10 paraphrased: The thief, Satan the father of all lies, comes only that he might disseminate his lies for the purpose of stealing our health, our peace, our relationships, our finances, and so on. To kill us as soon as possible, to destroy what God created us to be. But the Word came into the world to bring us truth, that through faith in the truth we may have a fulfilling life, a life filled with abundance from God so that we might live long and be satisfied. In so doing glorify our God.

God has left us in a world filled with deceptions of all kinds, and He expects us, as ambassadors of the Truth, to destroy those lies of the devil that is holding so many captive. Going forth we are to cast down those lies that we have exalted above God's Word. And after we have brought our life into obedience to the word, then we are to go after the lies that are working destruction in others, that they too may see the light of life and find shalom. Shalom is wholeness coming out of our covenant relationship with God.

2 Corinthians 10:4-6 For the weapons of our warfare are not carnal but mighty in God for pulling down strongholds, casting down arguments and every high thing that exalts itself against the knowledge of God, bringing every thought into captivity to the obedience of Christ, and being ready to punish all disobedience when your obedience is fulfilled. (NKJ)

The battle is; TRUTH vs. EVIL which side have we been on? Have we been promoting the truth of scripture or have we been passing on an evil report?

We need to put on the full armor of God which comes through intimacy with the word; because the devil will come against us with his lies in an attempt to make us believe that we are not really saved or that we are not the righteousness of God in Jesus. Or that we are powerless over the lies which come from the kingdom of darkness.

Ambassadors must put on the full armor for the sake of the kingdom! The armor of God is not only defensive but God designed it to be offensive; for we know that the best defense is a good active offense. Remember always that the Truth is the sword of the Spirit that will completely overpower any enemy.

THE GATES OF HELL ARE BUILT WITH WELL ESTABLISHED LIES.

As I was praying for a move of God upon our town, praying that God would tear down the strong holds that Satan had established in our area. It was then the Holy Spirit gave to me revelation into the power of the kingdom of darkness. He reveal that the gates of hell are only well established lies. Then He reminded me that the gates of hell cannot hold back the Church that is armed with the truth. We are the victors in Christ Jesus!

Matt 16:18 "And I also say to you that you are Peter, and on this rock I will build My church, and the gates of Hades shall not prevail against it. (NKJ) Upon the revelation of who Jesus is shall His Church be built, and the gates of Hades shall not prevail against it.

Most of the health report we hear today are designed by Satan to get us in fear. When we get in fear we are in position for the enemy to fulfill his destructive will in us and through us. Those who do not have faith in God's word are still reporting that there are giants in the land.

If our health was dependent upon what we ate or our environment then it would no longer depend upon God's Word. The Word said: If a believer were to drink anything deadly, it will by no means hurt them.

Remember what Luke 4:4 has taught us: Man shall not live by mere bread, but by every word of God. Faith in God's word creates for us realities that will protect us against harm. Read Psalm 91.

CAUTION: Do not go beyond what your faith can support, but be diligent about building your faith according to God's Word. Then never retreat from your faith that is firmly grounded in the Word of God.

How did Paul survive the bite of a poisonous snake? By faith in God's Word; that is by exalting spiritual law above natural law. **"Behold, I give you the authority to trample on serpents and scorpions, and over all the power of the enemy, and nothing shall by any means hurt you." Luke 10:19** (NKJ) The snake had no authority over Paul because he believed and did not doubt in his heart. The Word rules over the natural through our faith.

If you want to trust your health to what "they say" then you will eat the fruit of their wisdom.

Yesterday "they said" it was good to take plenty of vitamin E. Today "they say" it causes problems that can kill you. So who are you going to believe?

1 Tim 4:4-5 For every creature of God is good, and nothing is to be refused if it is received with thanksgiving; for it is sanctified by the word of God and prayer. (NKJ)

God has given us a weapon fit for its work; and that weapon is His Word and His Word is the standard for ALL TRUTH. His Word is our ROCK that cannot be shaken; those who hold fast to it are kept safe.

I heard a story about some fire fighters who were fighting a forest fire in the mountains. When it became evident that the fire would overtake them they were able to find shelter in the safety of a cave. But a life threatening situation arose. It happened as the fire drew near. The roar of the fire was like that of a freight train, causing some of the men to panic because of fright. Their fear that had been created by what they heard was enough to cause them to leave the safety of that cave. They would have ran from the safety of that cave to sure death had it not been for their leader. Their leader had to threaten them at gun point to keep them in the safety of that cave.

Will we run from our safe place when we are threatened? Or will we hold on all the tighter? The threats will come, and some will flee their safe place. Will you or will you be like the Psalmist? As the threats came against him, he declared: **"I will say of the LORD, "He is my refuge and my fortress; my God, in Him I will trust." Ps 91:2 (NKJ)**

There is no greater fortress than Jesus for He is Truth. Therefore, if we will commit to the Truth not fearing death, the world will see that we overcame because we did not depart from the truth. Amen

- There can only be one truth.
- Truth is not determined by popular opinion.
- Truth is truth and it can never be altered, that is the essence of truth.
- Truth will always stand the test of time.
- Truth is eternal.

A lie may appear to be true for it often takes on a reality. When those who seek truth find it, lies reality will be destroyed. Therefore, if you want to destroy lies realities take a strong grip on the truth and hold on, for victory is in your grasp.

As Jesus tells us in John chapter fifteen that we are called to abide in that truth, for if we do not abide in the truth we are not of Him. But if we abide in the truth we will over come the world for the god of this world is Satan and his kingdom is darkness. But Jesus has sent us into the world as light to set free those who have been held captive by darkness.

John 8:32 "And you shall know the truth, and the truth shall make you free." (NKJ)

If we say that we know Jesus but have not the truth in us we are a liar and a subject of the kingdom of darkness.

So who are they that overcome the world? **John 16:33 "These things I have spoken to you, that in Me you may have peace. In the world you will have tribulation; but be of good cheer, I have overcome the world." (NKJ)**

John 16:33 paraphrased: These things I have spoken to you, that in *Truth* you may have peace. In the world there will be tribulation; but be of good cheer, *Truth* has overcome the world.

Live in the Truth and live above the world and not beneath. If we do not accept the lies of the world we will not be under the power of the world. Thank you Jesus for you are the truth.

Satan fears those who live in the Truth for they have the power to destroy his kingdom because its foundation is lies.

REMEMBER, 2 Corinthians 10:4-6 For the weapons of our warfare are not carnal but mighty in God for pulling down strongholds, casting down arguments and every high thing that exalts itself against the knowledge of God, bringing every thought into captivity to the obedience of Christ, and being ready to punish all disobedience when your obedience is fulfilled. (NKJ)

Concluding statement for this chapter: Truth is a mighty weapon, it will pull down strongholds;

with it you can cast down arguments and every high thing that exalts itself against God's word. And with truth we can bring every thought into captivity to the obedience of Truth, and when we submit ourselves to the truth, we then will be able to take action against the kingdom of darkness.

1. There are only two spiritual kingdoms. **[Matthew 12:30]**
2. All mankind is under a spiritual kingdom. **[Matthew 12:30]**
3. There is the kingdom of light vs. the kingdom of darkness: Truth vs. Lies. **[John 10:10]**
4. Satan has been trying to discredit God's Word from the beginning. **[Genesis 3:1]**
5. A good report is a report that is in agreement with what God said. **[Numbers 14:36-37]**
6. A evil report is any report that goes against what God said. **[Numbers 13:30-33]**
7. We receive the fruit of what ever report we accept whether good or evil. **[Matthew 9:28-29]**
8. The destruction in the world has come through mankind believing Satan's lies. **[Genesis 3:17]**
9. Salvation comes through faith in God's Word. **[Romans 10:9]**

Bring Glory to God; use Jesus' authority to defeat every enemy that exalts itself against the Word of God!

CHAPTER SIX

BECOMING ONE WITH GOD

Ephesians 1:13 In Him *(Jesus)* **you also trusted, after you heard the word of truth, the gospel of your salvation; in whom also, having believed, you were sealed with the Holy Spirit of promise, (NKJ)**

Being baptized into the Name of Jesus is the act that seals us in a covenant relationship with Almighty God. It is when God says: You belong to Me because I give Myself to you.

This covenant is possible because God's love compelled Him to sacrifice His only begotten Son as payment for our sins, redeeming us from our sinful demise. Topping off that unprecedented mercy and grace He then through this same covenant of Love made us His sons, co-heirs with Jesus Christ, His only begotten. Clothing us with Jesus' righteousness He has enabled us to stand before our Heavenly Father without fault. Praise God!

As we look into what took place on the day of Pentecost we will see that the Church, the body of Christ, was baptized with the Holy Spirit. They were born again, born of the Spirit. That monumental, historical day God gave birth to Christ's body, the Church.

Luke 3:16 John *(the Baptist)* **answered, saying to all, "I indeed baptize you with water; but One mightier than I is coming, whose sandal strap I am not worthy to loose. He will <u>baptize</u> you with the Holy Spirit and fire. (NKJ)**

1 Corinthians 6:19-20 Or do you not know that your body is the temple of the Holy Spirit who is in you, whom you have from God, and you are not your own? For you were bought at a price; therefore glorify God in your body and in your spirit, which are God's. (NKJ)

Ephesians 1:13-14 In Him *(Jesus)* **you also trusted, after you heard the word of truth, the gospel of your salvation; in whom also, having believed, you were sealed with the Holy Spirit of promise, who is the guarantee of our inheritance until the redemption of the purchased possession, to the praise of His glory. (NKJ)**

When the Holy Spirit came upon the one hundred and twenty on the day of Pentecost they became spiritually alive empowering them to understand spiritual realities that were beyond them preceding the baptism with the Holy Spirit. With the revelation of the words that Jesus had spoken to them and the presents of the Holy Spirit they were able to operate in spiritual power beyond anything they had done prior. This baptism was what Jesus told them to wait for. And all of this was needful in establishing the kingdom of God on earth. This was for man's benefit and God's glory.

Luke 24:49 "Behold, I send the Promise of My Father upon you; but tarry in the city of Jerusalem until you are endued with power from on high." (NKJ) And through that act of baptism the one hundred and twenty who were gathered in that upper room that day were sealed into the Name of Jesus. Going forth in Jesus' authority empowered by the Holy Spirit proclaiming the good news "that the kingdom of God is at hand" and they did so with the demonstration of the authority that comes through faith in the name of Jesus. [1 Corinthians 2:4-5]

Through the power of the Holy Spirit three thousand believed and were added to their number that day. **Acts 2:1-4 Now when the Day of Pentecost <u>had fully come</u>, they were all with one accord in one place. And suddenly there came a sound from heaven, as of a rushing mighty wind, and it filled the whole house where they were sitting. Then there appeared to them divided tongues, as of fire, and one sat upon each of them. And they were all**

**filled with the Holy Spirit and began to speak with
other tongues, as the Spirit gave them utterance.
(NKJ)**

Jesus taught us that the feasts the Israelites prac-
ticed were types and shadows of things to come and
the feast of Pentecost (also called the feast of first
fruits) was no exception. From the first day that the
Israelites celebrated Pentecost up to the day that the
Holy Spirit come upon the one hundred and twenty
was a foretelling of that day, the day God would send
His Spirit creating the Church: that is Christ's body.

**Now when the Day of Pentecost had fully come,
...** The first fruits of Christ's Church were gathered
in and sealed by the Holy Spirit. **Acts 2:15-18 "For
these are not drunk, as you suppose, since it is only
the third hour of the day. "But this is what was
spoken by the prophet Joel: 'And it shall come
to pass in the last days, says God, that I will pour
out of My Spirit on all flesh; your sons and your
daughters shall prophesy, your young men shall
see visions, your old men shall dream dreams.
And on My menservants and on My maidservants I will pour out My Spirit in those days; and
they shall prophesy. (NKJ)** This was what John
the Baptist was referring to when he said: "He will
baptize you with the Holy Spirit and fire."

Right after receiving the baptism with the Holy
Spirit was when Peter addressed the crowd that had
asked: "What must we do to be saved?" **Acts 2:38
& 41: Then Peter said to them, "Repent, and let
every one of you be baptized in the name of Jesus
Christ for the remission of sins; and you shall**

receive the gift of the Holy Spirit. ... Then those who gladly received his word were baptized; and that day about three thousand souls were added to them. (NKJ)

I do believe that the baptism that the believers received that day was the baptism with the Holy Spirit the same baptism that the one hundred and twenty had just received. If it was water baptism, even at the rate of one baptism per minute it would have taken fifty hours to baptize three thousand souls. That would have taken at least four days, unless they baptized day and night, and then it would have taken more than two days. It says three thousand were baptized that day. When we do the math it leaves us with the Baptism with the Holy Spirit.

Through baptism God has become our Father and we have become co-heirs with His first born, His only begotten Son, Jesus. God our Father has through baptism with the Holy Spirit given us authority and the responsibility to conduct family business in the Name that we have now been identified with; that being the Name of Jesus. It was this seal that the followers of Jesus had to wait for that they might have the Kings authority to go out and minister in His Name. No seal, no authority.

In John fifteen Jesus tells us that if we are not one with Him we cannot do anything in His name. And without that baptism with the Holy Spirit we cannot be one with Him.

Romans 8:9-11 But you are not in the flesh but in the Spirit, if indeed the Spirit

of God dwells in you. Now if anyone does not have the Spirit of Christ, he is not His. And if Christ is in you, the body is dead because of sin, but the Spirit is life because of righteousness. But if the Spirit of Him who raised Jesus from the dead dwells in you, He who raised Christ from the dead will also give life to your mortal bodies through His Spirit who dwells in you. (NKJ) Because the Spirit of God lives in and through us our bodies are now instruments of life, not death.

LET US UNDERSTAND THIS NAME THAT WE HAVE BEEN BAPTIZED INTO.

There are some truths that we need to understand about the Name of Jesus for us to fully appreciate what it means to be baptized into that Name.

If we do not understand the origin of the Name of Jesus or how we receive the baptism with the Holy Spirit or what it means in the spiritual realm to be one with Jesus, then our baptism with the Holy Spirit will fail to do what God intend it to. That is to empower us to do the ministry of Jesus here on earth. If we do understand what takes place when we are baptized with the Holy Spirit it will empower us to minister with the authority that is in Jesus' Name. Jesus' Name is above all names because He has been appointed to God's right hand with the full authority of His Father's kingdom.

FIRST: WHAT IS THE ORIGIN OF THE NAME OF JESUS.

My understanding of the Name of Jesus began when I was studying what is commonly known as the Lord's Prayer: **Matt 6:9 "In this manner, therefore, pray: our Father in heaven, hallowed be Your name. (NKJ)**

It was at this point I asked the question of God: "If I am to hallow Your Name I need to know what Name that is?" So to the Word of God I went to find the answer.

Note: It said **"hallowed be Your name"** Name being singular, not names, so we are looking for a name.

Clue number one: **In Acts 4:12 it says: ... there is no other name under heaven given among men by which we must be saved." (NKJ)** Now I knew that the name that brings us salvation is the Name of Jesus.

Clue number two: In John seventeen Jesus testifies to the fact that He came in His Father's Name and Jesus asked that His Father would keep His disciples by the power of that Name. **John 17:6 & 11 "I have manifested Your name to the men whom You have given Me out of the world. They were Yours, You gave them to Me, and they have kept Your word. ..... "Now I am no longer in the world, but these are in the world, and I come to You. Holy Father, keep through Your name those whom You have given Me, that they may be one as We are. (NKJ)**

When Jesus said **"Holy Father, keep through Your name..."** He was speaking of the Name Jesus. Jesus is the Name by which we are kept. So the Name Jesus originated with God our Father. **"Holy Father, keep through <u>Your name</u> those whom You have given Me, that they may be one as We are." John 17:11b (NKJ)**

We receive the name Jesus when we become one with God through faith in the Word and the baptism with the Holy Spirit. Just like a husband and wife become one and share a common name, so it is with us. We are identified as being united with God by His Name. We have been sealed into an eternal covenant of love, resulting from our faith in Jesus. **[Isaiah 54:10]**

Ephesians 3:14- 15 For this reason I bow my knees to the Father of our Lord Jesus Christ, from whom <u>the whole family in heaven and earth is named,</u> (NKJ)

Now the union between a husband and wife is a union of the flesh. For it is said: "The two shall become one flesh". But the union between God and man is of the Spirit. Therefore, because the Spirit is eternal so is the union that takes place through baptism. This union is sealed when we are baptized with the Holy Spirit, and the two shall become one Spirit sharing a common name, Jesus. What God has joined together no man can separate. **[Romans 8:38-39]**

Ephesians 5:31-32 "For this reason a man shall leave his father and mother and be joined to his wife, and the two shall become one flesh." This is a great mystery, but I speak concerning Christ and the church. (NKJ)

When I conduct a wedding ceremony the last thing I do is present the couple as Mr. and Mrs. <u>Husband's last name</u>. In the ceremony of entering into a covenant relationship with God, after that intimate time of becoming one with God through the baptism with the Holy Spirit, we are presented to the spiritual realm as being identified by the name of Jesus.

In the covenant union between a husband and wife, the wife goes about after she has been married changing her name on her drivers license, social security card, bank account and so on.

Likewise when we have been baptized with the Holy Spirit into covenant with God we must go about changing our identity. And the first place we need to do so is in our own mind. We need to renew our mind, for if we do not view ourselves differently than we had prior to our entering into covenant with God we will continue to live out life not taking advantage of our covenant position in Christ. But if we renew our mind to the fact that we have been united with Christ having become one with God almighty, then we will act consistent with the view we have of ourselves. We will act like sons of God. Amen.

Proverbs 23:7a For as he thinks in his heart, so is he. (NKJ)

Jesus Christ was not the only one who came in that name, the Holy Spirit also came to us in the Name of Jesus. As we just read in [**Ephesians 3:14-15**] that the whole family <u>in heaven and earth</u> share a common Name.

Jesus said in **John 14:26 "But the Helper, the Holy Spirit, whom the Father will send <u>in My name,</u> He will teach you all things, and bring to your remembrance all things that I said to you. (NKJ)**

Now follow me: God is one and He has ONE name by which man can be united with Him and that name is Jesus; it is our family name. With that in mind we can look at these instructions to baptize believers understanding that they are both saying the same thing, there is no contradiction.

Matt 28:19-20 "Go therefore and make disciples of all the nations, baptizing them in the name of the Father and of the Son and of the Holy Spirit, "teaching them to observe all things that I have commanded you; and lo, I am with you always, even to the end of the age." Amen. (NKJ)

Acts 2:38-39 Then Peter said to them, "Repent, and let every one of you be baptized in the name of Jesus Christ for the remission of sins; and you shall receive the gift of the Holy Spirit. "For the promise

is to you and to your children, and to all who are afar off, as many as the Lord our God will call." (NKJ)

Whether it says, "baptizing them in the name of the Father and of the Son and of the Holy Spirit," OR "be baptized in the name of Jesus Christ" it is saying the same thing. One God, one Name, in which we share when we become one with Him.

The fact is that when we are baptized with the Holy Spirit in Jesus' Name; and that is the only way we can receive Him; we receive <u>the fullness of God</u>, Father, Son and Holy Spirit. This is very important to know in understanding what it means to be baptized into God's name.

John 14:23-26 Jesus answered and said to him, "If anyone loves Me, he will keep My word; and My Father will love him, and <u>We will come to him and make Our home with him</u>. "He who does not love Me does not keep My words; and the word which you hear is not Mine but the Father's who sent Me. "These things I have spoken to you while being present with you. "But the Helper, the Holy Spirit, whom the Father will send in My name, He will teach you all things, and bring to your remembrance all things that I said to you. (NKJ)

As the fullness of the God head was in Christ so it is with the Holy Spirit, He too is the fullness of the God head. **[Colossians 2:9]** Therefore the fullness of God is in us who have been united with God through the baptism with the Holy Spirit. **[Ephesians 1:22-23]**

> **Matt. 6:9b (NKJ) ... our Father in heaven, <u>hallowed be Your name</u> ...** *(JESUS)*

BAPTISM IDENTIFIES US WITH GOD.

There are many different baptisms and methods of baptism. There was the baptism into Moses: **1 Corinthians 10:2 all were baptized into Moses in the cloud and in the sea, (NKJ)**

There is Christ's baptism, the baptism of suffering for the gospels' sake: **Matt 20:22 But Jesus answered and said, "You do not know what you ask. Are you able to drink the cup that I am about to drink, and be baptized with the baptism that I am baptized with?" They said to Him, "We are able." (NKJ)**

There was the baptism of John the Baptist, a baptism with water: **Acts 19:4 Then Paul said, "John indeed baptized with a baptism of repentance, saying to the people that they should believe on Him who would come after him, that is, on Christ Jesus." (NKJ)**

And there is the baptism with the Holy Spirit that we are focusing on now. **Mark 1:8 "I indeed baptized you with water, but He will baptize you with the Holy Spirit." (NKJ)**

It is only through the baptism with the Holy Spirit that we are sealed into an eternal relationship with God. **Ephesians 4:30 And do not grieve the Holy Spirit of God, by whom you were sealed for the day of redemption. (NKJ)**

Water baptism does not seal us into a covenant relationship identifying us with Jesus. Water baptism is a ceremony that expresses our repentant heart. The fact is that a person can go through water baptism and never have entered into a covenant relationship with God because they did not receive the baptism with the Holy Spirit.

In the act of becoming married the man and woman goes through the ceremony of marriage, but if there is no consummation of that ceremony then there is no marriage.

To consummate is: To complete the marriage with the first act of sexual intercourse.

The ceremony is meaningless unless there is the act of the two becoming one flesh; likewise in entering into covenant with God.

In the New Testament when it refers to the Holy Spirit "falling upon" it is referring to the consummation of the Covenant with God. **Acts 10:44 While Peter was still speaking these words, the Holy Spirit fell upon all those who heard the word. (NKJ)** *fell upon; means:* to embrace with affection.

This first act of intimacy is when the Holy Spirit seals us in Covenant with God, when the two Spirits come together as one. In this act our relationship has been consummated; sealed.

Acts 19:2-6 he said to them, "Did you receive the Holy Spirit when you believed?" So they said to him, "We have not so much as heard whether there is a Holy Spirit." And he said to them, "Into what then were you baptized?" So they said, "Into John's baptism." Then Paul said, "John indeed baptized with a baptism of repentance, saying to the people that they should believe on Him who would come after him, that is, on Christ Jesus." When they heard this, they were baptized in the name of the Lord Jesus. And when Paul had laid hands on them, the Holy Spirit came upon them, and they spoke with tongues and prophesied. (NKJ)

For the most part people receive the Holy Spirit and are born again before they go through the ceremony of water baptism. It is because they have repented in their heart of their sinful ways and opened the way for the Spirit to come in.

Now I know that this teaching may go against what some of us have been taught, that being we receive the Holy Spirit when we are water baptized, but that is not what scripture declares.

Matt 3:11 *(John the Baptist speaking:)* **"I indeed baptize you with water unto repentance, but He who is coming after me is mightier than I, whose sandals I am not**

worthy to carry. He will baptize you with the Holy Spirit and fire. (NKJ)

Acts 8:14-17 Now when the apostles who were at Jerusalem heard that Samaria had received the word of God, they sent Peter and John to them, who, when they had come down, prayed for them that they might receive the Holy Spirit. For as yet He had fallen upon none of them. They had only been baptized.... (NKJ)

And further evidence that these are two separate acts can be found in the text we recently looked at: **Acts 19:2-6 he said to them, "Did you receive the Holy Spirit when you believed?" So they said to him, "We have not so much as heard whether there is a Holy Spirit." And he said to them, "Into what then were you baptized?" So they said, "Into John's baptism." Then Paul said, "John indeed baptized with a baptism of repentance, saying to the people that they should believe on Him who would come after him, that is, on Christ Jesus." When they heard this, they were baptized in the name of the Lord Jesus. And when Paul had laid hands on them, the Holy Spirit came upon them, and they spoke with tongues and prophesied. (NKJ)**

Remember you cannot receive what you do not know, for it is by faith that we receive from God. How can we believe for what we do not know? We cannot.

John the Baptist came to prepare the people by bringing them into repentance that they would be ready to receive Jesus. John the Baptist's ministry was to prepare the way of the Lord. The ONLY one who identifies us with Jesus is the one who was sent from God our Father in His Name, and He is the Holy Spirit.

Ephesians 1:13 In Him *(Jesus)* **you also trusted, after you heard the word of truth, the gospel of your salvation; in whom also, having believed, you were sealed with the Holy Spirit of promise, (NKJ)** No seal; no covenant relationship with God! And there is no intimacy with God outside of a covenant relationship. So if you want to become one with God because you believed the Word, you must do so by turning away from sin (repenting) and receive the baptism with the Holy Spirit. It is then you become the temple of God, you have become a vessel in whom the presence of God abides.

Romans 8:9a But you are not in the flesh but in the Spirit, if indeed the Spirit of God dwells in you. (NKJ)

WHAT TAKES PLACE IN THE SPIRITUAL REALM WHEN WE ARE BAPTIZED WITH THE HOLY SPIRIT INTO THE NAME OF JESUS'?

Spiritually we become one with Christ and receive authority to use the family name.

Romans 8:9b ... Now if anyone does not have the Spirit of Christ, he is not His. (NKJ) If we do not have the Spirit we do not have any authority under the Name of Jesus as this next scripture show.

> **Acts 19:13-16 Then some of the itinerant Jewish exorcists took it upon themselves to call the name of the Lord Jesus over those who had evil spirits, saying, "We exorcise you by the Jesus whom Paul preaches." Also there were seven sons of Sceva, a Jewish chief priest, who did so. And the evil spirit answered and said, "Jesus I know, and Paul I know; but who are you?" Then the man in whom the evil spirit was leaped on them, overpowered them, and prevailed against them, so that they fled out of that house naked and wounded. (NKJ)**

They knew about the authority that was in the Name of Jesus, BUT because they personally had not been identified with Jesus through the indwelling of the Holy Spirit, they were left void of any authority to use the Name of Jesus over demons. They only had the authority of man. Man without the Holy Spirit does not have authority over the demonic realm.

When we are baptized into the Name of Jesus we are translated into a new realm of authority. The Bible declares that we are NOW seated with Christ far above all principalities and powers.

As Spirit filled believers; we must understand that we have not been given authority only for the hereafter, but for the here and after.

Ephesians 2:4-6 But God, who is rich in mercy, because of His great love with which He loved us, even when we were dead in trespasses, made us alive together with Christ (by grace you have been saved), and raised us up together, and made us sit together in the heavenly places in Christ Jesus, (NKJ)

Now we know that when it says that we sit together with Christ Jesus in heavenly places it is speaking of our position of authority not of our physical presence. We have become one with Christ through baptism with the Holy Spirit; therefore we now have been elevated in authority, to Christ's authority. And through the presence of the Holy Spirit we are able to rule with the power of God's throne.

Ephesians 1:20-23 ... He raised Him from the dead and seated Him at His right hand in the heavenly places, far above all principality and power and might and dominion, and every name that is named, not only in this age but also in that which is to come. And He put all things under His feet, and gave Him to be head over all things to the church, which is His body, the fullness of Him who fills all in all. (NKJ)

Christ is the head of the Church, He is our authority, and we are to be the FULLNESS of Him who fills all in all.

Note: That fullness is in us even if no one ever manifests it. The manifestation can only happen if we allow the Spirit of God to rule in us and through us. Amen!

Now do not miss interpret what I am saying: We in no way are equal with God, for without Him we would not exist. But through the baptism with the Holy Spirit into the Name of Jesus, God has elevated us making us one with Him. That is God's plan and pleasure.

John 15:4-5 "Abide in Me, and I in you. As the branch cannot bear fruit of itself, unless it abides in the vine, neither can you, unless you abide in Me. "I am the vine, you are the branches. He who abides in Me, and I in him, bears much fruit; for without Me you can do nothing. (NKJ) That should make you want to shout. Hallelujah!

Jesus told the parable about the wayward son who took his inheritance, he then spent it on sinful living resulting in a life of lack. But when he came to his senses he went back to his father with the intent of getting a job as a servant, knowing his unworthiness to be called a son.

But the good news is; the father who had been waiting for him to return seen him coming afar off and went running to meet him. Throwing his arms around him he commanded that the servants bring a new robe and a ring for his finger and sandals for his feet. In so doing he restored his son with all rights as heir to the family name.

That is what God does when we return to Him recognizing our unworthiness: He dresses us with the robe of righteousness that belongs to Jesus and gives us His Name, His Spirit which is His signet ring making us heirs of the family Name. And He has given us His Word to stand on that we might live above this world, living a life that reflects our calling as the King's heirs.

Concluding statement: We who have been baptized with the Holy Spirit have received the name of Jesus with all its authority and responsibilities. The Holy Spirit was given to the Church on the day of Pentecost as a key part of God making His kingdom known here on earth.

1. Water baptism does not identify us with Jesus, it reflects our repentant heart. [**Acts 19:3-4**]
2. We are baptized into the Name of Jesus when we receive the Holy Spirit. [**Romans 8:9**]
3. All God's family in heaven and on earth has a common Name, Jesus. [**Ephesians 3:13-14**]
4. Without the baptism of the Holy Spirit we cannot conduct family business. [**Acts 19:13-16**]
5. It is the baptism with the Holy Spirit that causes rebirth in us. [**Acts 2:15-18**]

Bring Glory to God; use Jesus' authority to defeat every enemy that exalts itself against the Word of God!

CHAPTER SEVEN

WORD POWER

1 Pet 4:11a If anyone speaks, let him speak as the oracles of God. (NKJ)

Now we are at the crowning chapter of this book, the power of our words. This chapter is the nuts and bolts of ambassadorship. In this chapter we will see how we are able to do God's will on earth as it is in heaven. His will being that we rule as kings over those who oppose God's kingdom, that being Satan and all who do his will.

We overcome Satan by faith in the blood of the Lamb and by the word of our testimony. [**Rev 12:11**]

Imagine if you would that there were those who joined the armed forces, they were trained in all the disciplines needed to be a good soldier, with one exception; they were not taught how to use a weapon. They would look good marching but they sure would not last long in battle! That would not make much sense, would it? For without a weapon to defend and defeat the enemy all the rest would be of little value.

Well that is what has happened to most Christians. They have been trained in most disciplines of being Christ like, and Christ like we are called to be. **[Matt. 28:19]** But they have little or no training in using the sword of the Spirit.

> **Ephesians 6:17 And take the helmet of salvation, and the sword of the Spirit, which is the word of God; (NKJ)**

God's desire is that we would be well trained ministers of His Word, speaking it with a full expectation of it coming to pass. There are few who will take God at His Word; YET we are called to do just that, to the point of laying our life on the line. I pray that you are one who will trust God with your very life, for only then will you have the makings of a mighty king; one who is fully capable of handling the sword of the Spirit.

The Bible commands that those who are trained in Christ likeness are to speak with the full authority of God. **1 Pet 4:11a If anyone speaks, let him speak as the oracles of God. (NKJ)**

We MUST know that those who are living according to the Spirit of God and know the will of God have the authority and a mandate to speak on God's behalf. It is God's will for His children, His heirs, to be His ambassadors, representing His kingdom here on earth.

Acts 14:3 Therefore they stayed there a long time, speaking boldly <u>in</u> the Lord, who was bearing witness to the word of His grace, granting signs and wonders to be done by their hands. (NKJ)

The word translated <u>"in"</u> is the Greek word "epi" and it means = "on behalf of". They spoke boldly on behalf of the Lord. That is what an ambassador does!

To paraphrase Acts 14:3: Therefore they stayed there a long time, speaking boldly as ambassadors of the Lord, who was bearing witness to the word of His grace by granting signs and wonders which was done through ambassadors as they exercised their God given authority.

God does signs and wonders where there are those who will speak His word with a bold expectation. **Isaiah 44:24-26 Thus says the LORD, your Redeemer, and He who formed you from the womb: "I am the LORD, who makes all things, who stretches out the heavens all alone, who spreads abroad the earth by Myself; Who frustrates the signs of the babblers, and drives diviners mad; who turns wise men backward, and makes their knowledge foolishness; <u>Who confirms the word of His servant, and performs the counsel of His messengers:</u> (NKJ)**

What does it do for your faith to know; to truly know in your heart that God has given you authority to speak on His behalf as one who has inherited their authority from God's throne? Remember we are sons of God and co-heirs with Jesus. **[Romans 8:17]** If in deed we have His Spirit in us.

NOTE: Being a son of God is a position and is not gender specific. All who have been baptized into Jesus have become co-heirs with Him, male and female alike.

John 15:7-8 "If you abide in Me, and My words abide in you, you will ask what you desire, and it shall be done for you. "By this My Father is glorified, that you bear much fruit; so you will be My disciples. (NKJ)

It is not only a privilege but it is also a great responsibility, a responsibility that we will have to answer for when Jesus returns. He will ask: "What did you do with the authority I gave you?"

I pray believing that you are receiving revelation into what it means to be an ambassador. Even as I am writing this God is revealing more and more of what it means for me to be an ambassador for Christ. What it means to truly make God's word known in word and in deed.

Revelation 1:5-6 *(declares)* **... from Jesus Christ, the faithful witness, the firstborn from the dead, and the ruler over the kings of the earth. To Him who loved us and washed us from our sins in His own blood, and has made <u>us</u> kings and priests to His God and Father, to Him be glory and dominion forever and ever. Amen. (NKJ)**

God's ambassadors are the kings of the earth, with a king's call upon our life.

Anyone who knows anything about a king knows the king's authority is exercised through his word. If a king never gave an order he would have failed to exercise his kingly authority. We know that kings do give orders and when he does give an order it must be carried out in accordance with the king's authority. A mighty king has much authority but a lesser king has less authority.

In earlier chapters we have seen the great authority that we have in Christ, for Christ is the first born ruler over all creation, ruler over all that is seen and unseen. And the Bible declares that we are seated with Him far above all other principalities and powers. Praise God!

If we did not understand who the kings of the earth are in Revelation 1:5 we could falsely believe that it was talking about the rulers over the nations. But that is not who God considers to be the kings; the rulers of the earth. It is those who are in Christ that are the rulers of the earth in service to our God and Father. Once we understand who we are in Christ we will then rule as kings; that is ruling according to our words, knowing that God's army **[Psalms 103:20-21]** will carry out our commands given in the family Name; Jesus will see that they do.

1 Pet 4:11 If anyone speaks, let him speak as the oracles of God. If anyone ministers, let him do it as with the ability which God supplies, that in all things God may be

glorified through Jesus Christ, to whom belong the glory and the dominion forever and ever. Amen. (NKJ)

How did Jesus rule? He said to the storm; "Peace, be still" and He commanded the demons to leave, and to the lame; "Get up and walk." and for the dead to: "Get up." and to the sick; "Be healed." Jesus gave commands leaving us and example to follow for we are called to be Christ like.

Study the book of Acts to see how those who Jesus trained to be His ambassadors spoke commands in His name to the glory of God.

It is God who has chosen to make us a significant part of His kingdom, we did not earn the right, nor could we, we are what we are because of God's will and grace.

Isaiah 9:6-7 For unto us a Child is born, unto us a Son is given; and the government will be upon His shoulder. And His name will be called wonderful, Counselor, Mighty God, everlasting Father, Prince of Peace. Of the increase of His government and peace there will be no end, upon the throne of David and over His kingdom, to order it and establish it with judgment and justice from that time forward, even forever. The zeal of the LORD of hosts will perform this. (NKJ)

Ephesians 1:22-23 And He *(God)* **put all things under His** *(Jesus')* **feet, and gave Him to be head over all things to the church, which is His body, the <u>fullness</u> of Him who fills all in all. (NKJ)**

God has established a new ruling government whom Jesus is head and as we just read in Revelation 1:6 Jesus has declared that we are kings in His kingdom. As we have already seen: His kingdom is a spiritual kingdom that reigns over all other kingdoms whether spiritual or physical. God has declared that we are kings, therefore it can never be altered; it's irrevocable. We are the kings of the earth, sons of the living God.

I John 3:1a Behold what manner of love the Father has bestowed on us, that we should be called children of God! (NKJ)

We are of the royal line of the King of kings. We have more than a kingly spirit; we have the Spirit of the King of kings in us. We must let His Spirit reign through us.

AS YOU LOOK IN THE MIRROR SEE THE KING IN YOU; AND LET HIM REIGN!

2 Tim 1:7 For God has not given us a spirit of fear, but of power and of love and of a sound mind. (NKJ)

Why am I going into such detail about us being kings of the earth when this chapter is about the power of our words? It is because we were not born the King's kid. It was not until we were born again of the Spirit that we became heirs of the King of kings. So now we have to go through the process of learning how to rule as a king, to understand how much authority our words carry.

Remember: Jesus was crucified because he declared that He was a King, the Son of God. And if we dare take our rightful place in Christ as kings and sons of God we too will be rejected by some. But it is far better to be right in God's sight than to have the approval of man.

We can see a glimpse of a king's authority in the account of Daniel and the lion's den. The king did not want Daniel to be thrown into the lion's den but he had made a decree, his words had to be carried out.

Read Daniel chapter six for it will help you understand the authority of the word of a king. And our throne is far superior to any earthly throne for our throne is Christ's throne.

Rev 12:10-11 Then I heard a loud voice saying in heaven, "Now salvation, and strength, and the kingdom of our God, and the power of His Christ have come, for the accuser of our brethren, who accused them before our God day and night, has been cast down. "And they *(the Church - Christ's body - you)* **overcame him <u>by the blood of</u>**

the Lamb and **by the word of their testimony, and they did not love their lives to the death. (NKJ)**

The word translated "overcame" in the Greek is: nikao; and it means: to subdue and conquer.

Rev 12:12 paraphrased: "And the kings of the earth overcame all the schemes of the great deceiver and dominated him <u>by their faith in the blood of the Lamb and by the word of their testimony,</u> and they had no fear of death because they trusted their lives to the word of God.

It takes more than just our faith in the blood of the lamb for us to be conquers for Christ; it takes us speaking in faith as we trust completely in God's Word.

Oh that we may understand how important it is for us to see ourselves in the high position the King of kings has placed us in. He has anointed us with His Spirit to be kings in His spiritual kingdom, to reign over this natural world supernaturally through our faith connection to His throne.

Because we have been anointed with the Holy Spirit we have the very nature of the King of kings in us, and we are called to obey that Kingly Spirit. Romans 8:14 For as many as are led by the Spirit of God, these are sons of God. (NKJ)

The fact that we are God's sons makes us royalty, with royal responsibilities.

Being made a king in God's kingdom was not for the purpose of entertainment; but be assured it is a work that we can enjoy doing. To see all God's enemies being made His footstool, what a great pleasure that is for those who love God.

The account of Joseph and the Pharaoh will help us understand our authority in Christ as rulers in God's kingdom, and how much authority God has given to what we say.

Genesis 41:39-44 Then Pharaoh said to Joseph, "Inasmuch as God has shown you all this, there is no one as discerning and wise as you. "You shall be over my house, and all my people <u>shall be ruled according to your word</u>; only in regard to the throne will I be greater than you." And Pharaoh said to Joseph, "See, I have set you over all the land of Egypt." Then Pharaoh took his signet ring off his hand and put it on Joseph's hand; and he clothed him in garments of fine linen and put a gold chain around his neck. And he had him ride in the second chariot which he had; and they cried out before him, "Bow the knee!" So he set him over all the land of Egypt. Pharaoh also said to Joseph, "I am Pharaoh, and without your consent no man may lift his hand or foot in all the land of Egypt." (NKJ)

Here we have the Pharaoh who is the supreme authority over the land of Egypt, and His signet ring which embodies the Pharaoh's authority. Anyone who legally possessed the Kings signet ring possessed the Kings authority.

And for us the Holy Spirit is God's signet ring, His seal. Those who have the Holy Spirit have been given God's legal authority to act on His behalf.

From the time Pharaoh put Joseph in charge of his entire kingdom nothing could be done unless Joseph gave his consent. **"You shall be over my house, and all my people <u>shall be ruled according to your word</u>;"** Joseph did not have authority over the Pharaoh, but he was put in charge by Pharaoh over all that Pharaoh had authority over. Do you see the likeness?

Genesis 41:55 So when all the land of Egypt was famished, the people cried to Pharaoh for bread. Then Pharaoh said to all the Egyptians, "<u>Go to Joseph</u>; <u>whatever he says</u> to you, do." (NKJ)

Everything in the land of Egypt was dependent upon what Joseph said, the Pharaoh would not interfere; he gave his word. Likewise here on this earth God has put His ambassadors over His affairs. It is according to our consent that things happen concerning God's kingdom on Earth.

There is a tremendous famine in the land today! And God's storehouse is full of provisions; so where are the Josephs to authorize the release?

Matt 24:44-47 "Therefore you also be ready, for the Son of Man is coming at an hour you do not expect. "Who then is a faithful and wise servant, whom his master made ruler over his household, to give them food in due season? "Blessed is that servant whom his master, when he comes, will find so doing. "Assuredly, I say to you that he will make him ruler over all his goods. (NKJ)

Jesus said in **Matt 18:19 "Again I say to you that if two of you agree on earth concerning anything that they <u>ask</u>, it will be done for them by My Father in heaven. (NKJ)** That is why it is so important for us to put a guard over our mouth; that we only say what is in agreement with God's will, God's Word.

We are not here as rulers to fulfill our own personal agenda, but we are here as ambassadors of the kingdom of God. Like Jesus we are to only speaking the will of the One in whose Name we represent.

Gen. 41:39-40 Then Pharaoh said to Joseph, "Inasmuch as God has shown you all this, there is no one as discerning and wise as you. "You shall be over my house, and all my people <u>shall be ruled according to your word</u>. (NKJ)

"Inasmuch as God has shown you all this" Authority comes through revelation of God's word, the more revelation we have of God's will the more authority we have been given. And Jesus said to the one who has been given little, little is required, but to the one who has been given much, much is required. The more we know the more we need to do in Jesus name.

Jesus said: **"Most assuredly, I say to you, he who receives whomever I send receives Me; and he who receives Me receives Him who sent Me." John 13:20 (NKJ)**

We have been sent into this world to do what Jesus would do, the way Jesus would do it. Amen!

Genesis 1:26-27 Then God said, "Let Us make man in Our image, according to Our likeness; <u>let them have dominion</u> over the fish of the sea, over the birds of the air, and over the cattle, over all the earth and over every creeping thing that creeps on the earth." So God created man in His own image; in the image of God He created him; male and female He created them. (NKJ)

It is necessary for us to come back to the creation of mankind that we might understand what it means to be created in the image and likeness of God. We will not fully grasp the concept of ruling according to our words; ruling in the God like manner unless we do.

UNDERSTAND: Our words rule; and they are going to produce fruit whether we comprehend the authority given to our spoken word or not.

There are those who are highly trained in the marshal arts and their hands are considered lethal weapons, but I am declaring to you now that our words in accordance to what we believe has far more power than any weapon, that is weapons of the natural realm. Our faith filled words are spiritual, having supernatural power; they can move a mountain.

2 Corinthians 10:4-6 For the weapons of our warfare are not carnal but mighty in God for pulling down strongholds, casting down arguments and every high thing that exalts itself against the knowledge of God, bringing every thought into captivity to the obedience of Christ, and being ready to punish all disobedience when your obedience is fulfilled. (NKJ)

I had stated in an earlier chapter that when it says that we were created in His image and likeness it was not speaking about our physical appearance for God is Spirit. What it is telling us is that we were created to be like God in our being and doing, we are spiritual beings clothed in flesh to reign over the earth realm.

We were created to reflect who God is: **2 Corinthians 3:18 But we all, with unveiled face, beholding as in a mirror the glory of the Lord, <u>are being transformed into the same image</u> from**

glory to glory, just as by the Spirit of the Lord. (NKJ) Praise God!

Jesus is the express image of God: Philip said to Jesus: "Show us the Father." And Jesus replied: "If you have seen Me you have seen the Father."

Now it is our responsibility to bear the image of Jesus: **1 Corinthians 15:49 And as we have borne the image of the man of dust, we shall also bear the image of the heavenly Man. (NKJ)**

And in **[Ephesians 1:22-23]** it declares that in the Church there should be seen the fullness of Christ.

Jesus has demonstrated to us how to rule in the kingdom of Heaven and we are called to follow His example: **Matt 28:19-20 "Go therefore and make disciples of all the nations, baptizing them in the name of the Father and of the Son and of the Holy Spirit, teaching them to observe all things that I have commanded you; and lo, I am with you always, even to the end of the age." Amen. (NKJ)**

"Go therefore and make disciples ..." A disciple is one who follows in the way of his master. And in **John 14:12-13 Jesus said: "Most assuredly, I say to you, he who believes in Me, the works that I do he will do also; and greater works than these he will do, because I go to My Father. And whatever you ask in My name, that I will do, that the Father may be glorified in the Son." (NKJ)**

Jesus was talking about those who have His Spirit; His character and believes in the authority of the Word, would do the SAME WORKS the SAME WAY Jesus did. Too often we want the same results but we do not operate in the same authority. We simply do not know or do not believe what the Word says.

The word that has been translated *ask* in John 14:13 is also translated: "call for" and call for would have been a better choice here for as we look at how Jesus' disciples operated we see how they called in Jesus' Name for something to be done and it was done.

Example: **Acts 3:6-8 Then Peter said, "Silver and gold I do not have, but what I do have I give you: In the name of Jesus Christ of Nazareth, rise up and walk." And he took him by the right hand and lifted him up, and immediately his feet and ankle bones received strength. So he, leaping up, stood and walked and entered the temple with them—walking, leaping, and praising God. (NKJ)**

And: **Acts 14:8-10 And in Lystra a certain man without strength in his feet was sitting, a cripple from his mother's womb, who had never walked. This man heard Paul speaking. Paul, observing him intently and seeing that he had faith to be healed, said with a loud voice, "Stand up straight on your feet!" And he leaped and walked. (NKJ)**

Notice that Paul did not say: In the name of Jesus; because Paul understood that he had been baptized into the name of Jesus and all that he did was in Jesus' name. **[Col.3:17]**

There are many more examples of calling for but I think you get the picture; whatever you call for in Jesus' name, that He will do, that the Father may be glorified in the Son.

When Jesus calmed the storm He did not take an oar and beat down the waves; NO He spoke to the waves. He said: "Peace, be still!" And the sea became calm. That is kingly authority; that is a King exercising dominion over His domain.

You are a king, so do you know what your domain is? Christ's domain is our domain just like the Pharaoh's domain was Joseph's domain.

How do you think the Pharaoh would have felt if Joseph would not have used the authority given him; the authority of the Pharaoh to rule Egypt?

How do you think God feels when we do not use His authority that He bestowed upon us?

How often is God spoken badly of because His ambassadors, those who have been put in charge of the affairs of the kingdom did not use the authority given them to defeat God's enemies?

We are called to rule like God, and He rules: "by the word of His power" **Hebrews 1:1-3 God, who at various times and in various ways spoke in time past to the fathers by the prophets, has in these last days spoken to us by His Son, whom He has appointed heir of all things, through whom also He made the worlds; who being the brightness of His glory and the express image of His person, and upholding all things by the word of His power, when He had by Himself purged our sins, sat down at the right hand of the Majesty on high, (NKJ)**

"upholding all things by the word of His power," Another translation for the word, translated upholding is "bring forth" Bringing forth all things by the word of His power. His power to bring forth is connected to His word. Therefore our power to bring forth is connect to our word, for we were created like Him and empowered by His Spirit.

We see God bringing forth by the word of His power throughout creation: **Genesis 1:3 Then God said, "Let there be light"; and there was light.** And there is still light!

In John chapter one it tells us that all that was made was made through the spoken word of God, and outside of the spoken word was nothing made. John 1:1-4 In the beginning was the Word, and the Word was with God, and the Word was God. He was in the beginning with God. All things were made through Him, and without Him nothing was made that was made. In Him was life, and the life was the light of men. (NKJ)

So as we understand that God does nothing outside of the spoken word, and we know that we were made by God to be like God, that is in our being and doing, we then can start to understand what authority has been given to our spoken words. Amen.

Jesus said to His followers: **"For assuredly, I say to you, <u>whoever says</u> to this mountain, 'Be removed and be cast into the sea,' and does not doubt in his heart, but believes that those things <u>he says</u> will come to pass, <u>he will have whatever he says</u>. Mark 11:23 (NKJ)**

How are we instructed to bring things about? By saying and not doubting, to be like God in our doing and being.

Note: Because we were made in God's image and likeness, we create according to our faith filled words. Remember this authority can be used for good or evil! This is how new diseases come into existence. Today we hear all kinds of prophesying about the bird flu and West Nile's disease and so on. This kind of talk comes out of fear and not out of faith in God's Word. As Christ's ambassadors we are called to proclaim the Good News that sets people free, heals the sick and so on.

PLEASE UNDERSTAND THIS: When we speak we are placing a demand upon the spirit realm to produce a physical result. This is what God has ordained for His children.

Mark 9:23 Jesus said to him, "If you can believe, all things are possible to him who believes." (NKJ)

Jesus' disciples ask why they could not cast the evil spirit out of a boy and Jesus said: "because of your unbelief." They were speaking; but they did not believe. **Matt 17:19-20 Then the disciples came to Jesus privately and said, "Why could we not cast him out?" So Jesus said to them, "Because of your unbelief; for assuredly, I say to you, if you have faith as a mustard seed, you will say to this mountain, 'Move from here to there,' and it will move; and nothing will be impossible for you. (NKJ)**

So what is impossible for a man of faith? Nothing! Take Joshua, he spoke to the sun and it did not go down for a full day. **Josh 10:12-13 Then Joshua spoke to the LORD in the day when the LORD delivered up the Amorites before the children of Israel, and he said in the sight of Israel: "Sun, stand still over Gibeon; and Moon, in the Valley of Aijalon." So the sun stood still, and the moon stopped, till the people had revenge upon their enemies. Is this not written in the Book of Jasher? So the sun stood still in the midst of heaven, and did not hasten to go down for about a whole day. (NKJ)**

Now that is kingly authority! That is being and doing in the image and likeness of our creator God.

NOTE: Joshua was not speaking to the Lord but for the Lord when he told the sun and moon to stand still.

Do you see the same spiritual law at work here as in **Mark 11:23 "For assuredly, I say to you, whoever says to this mountain, 'Be removed and be cast into the sea,' and does not doubt in his heart, but believes that those things he says will come to pass, he will have whatever he says. (NKJ)**

As humans our faith and our words are tied together. The Word of God teaches us that out of our heart the mouth speaks and produces.

Matt 12:34-35 "Brood of vipers! How can you, being evil, speak good things? For out of the abundance of the heart the mouth

speaks. "A good man out of the good treasure of his heart brings forth good things,
and an evil man out of the evil treasure
brings forth evil things. (NKJ)

The key words in this text are heart, speaks and
brings forth. When we speak what is in our heart we
bring forth; that is to create according to our words.
A good man out of the treasure of his heart brings
forth good things in accordance with what he says,
and an evil man out of the evil treasure of his heart
brings forth evil things in accordance with what he
says.

Ps 119:11 Your word I have hidden in my heart,
that I might not sin against You! (NKJ) Oh that my
heart might be full of God's word that I would bring
forth only good things with my words.

Can you see that the greatest muscle we have
is our tongue? It can do more good or evil than all
the rest of the body put together. Our tongue has the
power to move mountains when we believe what
we say. This spiritual law does not just apply only
to mountains, it applies to everything we say and
believe.

What ever you say if you do not doubt in your
heart, but believe that those things you say will come
to pass, you will have whatever you say. This is
God's law!

James 3:10 Out of the same mouth proceed
blessing and cursing. My brethren, these things
ought not to be so. (NKJ) Let us stop and put a
guard over our mouths. Amen.

Remember: Spiritual laws can work for us or against us depend upon what we believe and say.

Proverbs 18:20-21 A man's stomach shall be satisfied from the fruit of his mouth, from the produce of his lips he shall be filled. Death and life are in the power of the tongue, and those who love it will eat its fruit. (NKJ)

I believe when we understand what power God has ordained for our tongue we can learn to love it and use it to bring forth good fruit that will please God and satisfy us.

James has much to say about the power of the tongue: **James 3:2-12 For we all stumble in many things. If anyone does not stumble in word, he is a perfect man, able also to bridle the whole body. Indeed, we put bits in horses' mouths that they may obey us, and we turn their whole body. Look also at ships: although they are so large and are driven by fierce winds, they are turned by a very small rudder wherever the pilot desires. Even so the tongue is a little member and boasts great things. See how great a forest a little fire kindles! And the tongue is a fire, a world of iniquity. The tongue is so set among our members that it defiles the whole body, and sets on fire the course of nature; and it is set on fire by hell. For every kind of beast and bird, of reptile and creature of the sea, is tamed and has been tamed by mankind. But no man can tame the tongue. It is an unruly** evil, full of deadly poison. **With it we bless our God and Father, and with it we curse men, who have been made in the similitude of God. Out of the same mouth proceed blessing and cursing. My brethren, these things ought not to be so. Does a spring send forth fresh water and bitter from the same opening? Can a fig tree, my brethren, bear olives, or a grapevine bear figs? Thus no spring can yield both salt water and fresh. (NKJ)**

Why are we instructed to be slow to speak? That we might think through what we say; for it is in the mind that we are to take every thought captive and bring it into obedience to the Word of God. For when we do speak we decree what ever we say because we are kings with kingly authority.

James emphasizes over and over how the tongue has dominion over the whole body.

- If a man can control his tongue he can bless his whole body.
- It is a fact that words will either bless or curse.
- By our words we will be judged.

James 3: 4 Look also at ships: although they are so large and are driven by fierce winds, they are turned by a very small rudder wherever the pilot desires. (NKJ) The ship has <u>no choice</u> but to respond to the rudder even though it is so small in size compared to the large ship, likewise James is telling us, our body has <u>no choice</u> but to respond to what our tongue is saying.

The way to put yourself under a curse is to say such things as: "Well, you know we live in a fallen world and so we have to expect that bad things will happen to us. We're not special you know." Those are words given to us by the devil himself. If we have been speaking in this way we need to repent and start speaking blessings instead of curses.

We are special because we have a covenant relationship with God. Therefore we are in the world but we are not of the world nor are we subject to the curses of those who are of the world. The world may war against us but in Christ it will never conquer us. Amen.

In 1 Samuel 14:6 Jonathan explained to his young friend that God distinguishes between those who are in covenant with Him and those who have no covenant.

1 Samuel 14:6 Then Jonathan said to the young man who bore his armor, "Come, let us go over to the garrison of these uncircumcised *(those who have no covenant with God)*; **it may be that the LORD will work for us. For nothing restrains the LORD from saving by many or by few." (NKJ)**

2 Corinthians 10:4 For the weapons of our warfare are not carnal but mighty in God for pulling down strongholds, (NKJ)

The weapons of our warfare are our faith filled words. God's law says that what ever we say and believe in our heart we will have. And we speak according to God's will, for we are His ambassadors.

I know that God shows favor to those in covenant with Him because of the way He protected the Israelites. He protected them from the ten plagues of Egypt and when God led the Israelite out of Egypt it say that there was not one feeble one among them.

Psalms 105:37 He also brought them out with silver and gold, and there was none feeble among His tribes. (NKJ)

God's desire is to keep us according to His Covenant, His Word. But for that to become a reality in our life we must believe and therefore speak God's covenant promises into our lives. For God's saving grace comes through believing God's Word and confessing with our mouth.

Romans 10:10 For with the heart one believes unto righteousness, and with the mouth confession is made unto salvation. (NKJ)

Too often we limit God's salvation to the saving of our soul and eternal life, but God's salvation is so much more if we will believe and confess what God has promised us. [Ephesians. 3:17-21]

Deuteronomy 28:2-14 "And all these blessings shall come upon you and overtake you, because you obey the voice of the LORD your God:

"Blessed shall you be in the city, and blessed shall you be in the country.

"Blessed shall be the fruit of your body, the produce of your ground and the increase of your herds, the increase of your cattle and the offspring of your flocks.

"Blessed shall be your basket and your kneading bowl.

"Blessed shall you be when you come in, and blessed shall you be when you go out. "The LORD will cause your enemies who rise against you to be defeated before your face; they shall come out against you one way and flee before you seven ways. "The LORD will command the blessing on you in your storehouses and in all to which you set your hand, and He will bless you in the land which the LORD your God is giving you. "The LORD will establish you as a holy people to Himself, just as He has sworn to you, if you keep the commandments of the LORD your God and walk in His ways. "Then all peoples of the earth shall see that you are called by the name of the LORD, and they shall be afraid of you. "And the LORD will grant you plenty of goods, in the fruit of your body, in the increase of your livestock, and in the produce of your ground, in the land of which the LORD swore to your fathers to give you. "The LORD will open to you His good treasure, the heavens, to give the rain to your land in its season, and to bless all the work of your hand. You shall lend to many nations, but you shall not borrow. "And the LORD will make you the head and not the tail; you shall be above only, and not be beneath, if you heed the commandments of the LORD your God, which I command you today, and are careful to observe them. "So you shall not turn aside from any of the words which I command you this day, to the right hand or to the left, to go after other gods to serve them. (NKJ)

2 Corinthians 1:20 For all the promises of God in Him are Yes, and in Him Amen, to the glory of God through us. (NKJ)

Now can you see that there is much more to God's salvation than just eternal life? That alone would be a great salvation package. But God wants to be glorified and praised because of His many blessings He gives to those who will believe for them.

Ps 103:1-5 Bless the LORD, O my soul; and all that is within me, bless His holy name! Bless the LORD, O my soul, and forget not all His benefits: Who forgives all your iniquities, who heals all your diseases, Who redeems your life from destruction, who crowns you with lovingkindness and tender mercies, <u>Who satisfies your mouth with good things</u>, so that your youth is renewed like the eagle's. (NKJ) He gives you good promises to speak into your life that will cause your youth to be renewed like the eagle's. Have you been speaking His blessings or the curses of this world?

Remember: **Luke 6:45 "A good man out of the good treasure of his heart brings forth good; and an evil man out of the evil treasure of his heart brings forth evil. For out of the abundance of the heart his mouth speaks. (NKJ)**

If there is any unbelief in your heart, guard your mouth so that you do not speak it. Then renew your mind according to God's Word until it produces faith in your heart. When faith has come, open your mouth and receive what has been promise by God. Take God at His Word! He will not let you down.

Hosea 14:2 Take words with you, and return to the LORD. Say to Him, "Take away all iniquity; receive us graciously, for we will offer the sacrifices of our lips. (NKJ) We are to offer our lips to God for speaking out His praises and will. Amen.

II Thessalonians 1:11-12 Therefore we also pray always for you that our God would count you worthy of this calling, and fulfill all the good pleasure of His goodness and the work of faith with power, that the name of our Lord Jesus Christ may be glorified in you, and you in Him, according to the grace of our God and the Lord Jesus Christ. (NKJ)

Concluding statement: We were made in the image and likeness of God our creator to be like Him in our being and doing, and God rules by the Word of His power. Therefore we also rule according to the authority given to our words producing either good or evil, depending upon what is in our heart and to whose throne we are connected; God's or Satan's.

Words without authority are useless; but words spoken with authority are as strong as the authority behind them. The authority behind our words is God's throne.

1. God created all things according to His spoken Word. [**John 1:1-3**]
2. God ordained that man rule the earth as kings. [**Revelation 1:6**]
3. Out of the heart the mouth speaks producing good or evil. [**Matthew 12: 34-35**]
4. The tongue has controlling power over the body. [**James 3**]
5. Even death and life are in the power of the tongue. [**Proverbs 18:21**]
6. We will be judged by our words. [**Matthew 12:36**]

Bring Glory to God; use Jesus' authority to defeat every enemy that exalts itself against the Word of God!

CONCLUSION

There is so much more that can be said on the subject of being God's representative to planet earth. But I do believe that with the help of the Holy Spirit and the Word of God, I have laid a biblical foundation as to the call upon God's ambassadors; those sent in the Name of Jesus; and to the importance of receiving God's provisions through the man of God. **John 13:20 "Most assuredly, I say to you, he who receives whomever I send receives Me; and he who receives Me receives Him who sent Me." (NKJ)**

If we receive the ambassador of God in Jesus name it is the same as receiving God Himself. BUT if we do not receive those sent in Jesus' name we are rejecting the sender.

Therefore; let those who are mature in the faith represent Jesus in His fullness; with moral integrity and spiritual authority. And to those who are in need of a touch from God; let them seek out an ambassador of Jesus that they might receive from God through them. When I need a touch from God, I do what I am asking you to do; I seek out a man of God to speak a blessing into my life. I believe in the authority of God's ambassadors.

> **Jude 1:24-25 Now to Him who is able to keep you from stumbling, and to present you faultless before the presence of His glory with exceeding joy, To God our Savior, who alone is wise, be glory and majesty, dominion and power, both now and forever. Amen.**
> **(NKJ)**

Printed in the United States
90282LV00001BB/1-168/A